BO McMILLIN

Man and Legend

Charles W. Akers
and
John W. Carter

THE SULGRAVE PRESS · LOUISVILLE, KENTUCKY

The Publisher wishes to give thanks for the contributions of Hayden Edwards, Jack Kannapell and William Swearingen to this book and to Centre College and Indiana University alumni associations for their assistance in providing information and photographs.

Contents

Acknowledgments

This book had its origin in 1975 when Charles Akers was invited to contribute an article on Bo McMillin for the *Dictionary of American Biography* and soon discovered how much of the life of the fabulous "Bo" was hidden in legend. The extensive research required to complete the article suggested the need for a biography, but this project languished until 1984, when John Carter undertook the responsibility of completing the research and writing the chapters beginning with McMillin's move to Indiana University in 1934.

In pursuing the McMillin story through institutional archives and endless newspaper files, we have acquired large debts of gratitude. Kathryn Gillihan McMillin made available a collection of memorabilia concerning her late husband and authorized access to his academic and military records. His sister, Katherine McMillin Sherrod, patiently answered frequent queries concerning the family. Kay Minton Hollingsworth loaned a copy of the *Lasso,* the North Side Fort Worth High School yearbook, that had belonged to her father, Rosco Minton. John Y. Brown, Sr. contributed a copy of his book, *The Legend of the Praying Colonels,* the largest collection of stories about the Centre team, and gave our work his blessing. It is unfortunate that Brown's material for a second book on Centre College was lost before it could be published.

Robert E. Glass of the Grace Doherty Library of Centre College provided full access to the College's archives and special collections. While working on a history of athletics at Centenary College, George W. Treese generously shared the results of his research on McMillin's years in Shreveport. Diane Kaplan and Carolyn Garison, archivists of Centenary College, searched their collections for McMillin items. For Geneva College, we depended on the searches of William H. Russell, professor of history and former dean. Archivists Tony Crawford and Shirley J. Serrault of Kansas State University supplied numerous documents and publications. Kit Klingelhoffer, Sports Information Director of Indiana University, was most helpful in locating Athletic Department records and patiently answering questions. The staff of the Indiana University Archives, especially Archivist Dolores M. Lehrman, gave invaluable access to Board records and correspondence. Barbara K. Somerville of Oakland University's Kresge Library made a major contribution by locating and obtaining on Interlibrary Loan microfilm files of newspapers.

In an effort to capture the essence of Bo McMillin that escaped the written page, we have consulted in one form or another his surviving friends, players, and associates. The taped interviews, questionnaires, and letters in our files preserve the memories of those who worked most closely with this man they almost unanimously characterize as "unforgettable." We are especially indebted to Governor Albert B. Chandler, who shared with us the memories of his life-long friendship with Bo. Regretfully, we can only list the many others: Carl R. Anderson, Edwin J. Anderson, E. Antonini, Eldon Auker, Emmett Breen, Mary Minton Callanan, James M. Campbell, David E. Cullen, Chris Dal Sasso, Roy Dumke, A. R. Edward, Howard C. Emrick, Paul "Pete" Fairbank, Lud C. Fiser, O.H. "Buck" Fletcher, Dwight Gahm, Ralph Graham, Robert Haak, Leon Hart, Harry J. Haude, R. Calvin Hubbard, Adolph R. Hraba, R. L. Kenderdine, W. Nick Kerbawy, Bobby Layne, Joseph Limes, Roy Macklem, Archie M. McSparrin, Robert Mann, Ernest H. Meyer, Louis Mihajlovich, Thomas Miller, Sherman A. Minton, Kenneth Moeller, L. W. Newcomer, Alexander Nigro, Pete Pihos, Howard Pinkerton, Del Russell, Lou Saban, Clyde B. Smith, Franklin H. Smith, Alvin Stephenson, George Taliaferro, Russell Thomas, James Trimble, Doak Walker, and Walter W. Zeckser.

To whatever degree we have captured the spirit of Bo McMillin, it is due these who have recounted for us their association with him.

Prologue

"Colonel" Dave Egan, the noted sports columnist of the *Boston Daily Record,* refused to believe the news he read in April 1952:

> It says in the newspapers that Alvin "Bo" McMillin has died, but this is an exaggeration. He has not died, and he will not die, so long as there lives one man among us who witnessed the Harvard-Centre football classics in 1920 and 1921.

Like Egan, two generations of Americans had cherished the legend of Alvin Nugent "Bo" McMillin, the giant-killing folk hero, the champion of the common man against the elite, and the South and West against the East. In 1921 the "Praying Colonels" of little Centre College of Kentucky defeated Harvard University, the nation's mightiest football power. The shock was so great that fifty years later the *New York Times* still hailed Centre's victory as "football's upset of the century."

This triumph in Harvard Stadium climaxed three years during which the "Praying Colonels," with McMillin as their fabled quarterback, taught colleges throughout the nation that a small school could rise to fame and glory by recruiting a few outstanding athletes. Much of the country had been caught up in Centre's two-year David and Goliath struggle against the Ivy League champion. Even before he scored the touchdown that beat Harvard in 1921, the deeply religious McMillin had been elevated from the stature of All-American player to mythic hero in a popular book for boys that fictionalized his rise from poverty and delinquency to personification of the highest values of American society. Until Red Grange began his climb to gridiron immortality two years later, this Texan who had played for a tiny Kentucky college was the most talked about, best known football player in the United States.

When Bo McMillin moved from playing to coaching, his legend continued to grow as those who had known him repeated and enlarged stories of his prowess and unique personality. His greatness on the gridiron, reported on thousands of newspaper pages, was matched in legend by tales of amazing feats elsewhere. Admirers insisted that he could roll dice "from two up to twelve and then from twelve back down to two," could tell the exact time without a clock when awakened at any hour of the night, or could swim over waterfalls or upstream against the swiftest current. His influence over his teammates was reputed to be so great that he persuaded one of them to have a crooked finger cut off to better catch the football. Thus, as a reporter once noted, "Stories about Bo McMillin flow on and on, some of them hilarious, some of them solemn. On every side you hear fresh crops of them, because the man was the sort of personality phenomenon whose simplest act becomes legend. His most intimate friends will never know all the interesting, humorous, comforting tales about Bo. But they will go on collecting them and recounting them as long as they live."

While still a player, McMillin had begun to contribute to his own legend by acting the part the press attributed to him. In time he stopped acting; the man and the legend became one. As a coach he delighted in telling his players how football had kept him from being a tramp or worse, how the Praying Colonels had slain the Crimson giant, and how his "pore lil' boys" could also win in both football and life through hard work, clean living, and sportsmanship. In the small colleges where he coached at first — by choice, he said — his players accepted their legendary leader in full faith and nearly matched his feats.

When he moved on to major coaching positions, the victories came harder but his heroic aura remained strong. Then in 1945 the legend of Bo McMillin the giant killer was reborn when he led Indiana University to its first Big Ten Championship. An early death robbed him of the opportunity to test fully whether the values enshrined in his life could be transferred from college to the professional game.

Unlike many of the sport heroes of the 1920s, fact and fiction were not far apart in the life of Bo McMillin. Stripped of its few fantasies and frequent slight exaggerations, his story remains genuinely heroic. He was the rare hero in whom character was as important as athletic ability. The legend he attempted to live was a sermon in action for an age of rapid change and excesses, a homily that may have reached a wider audience of youth than the exhortations of the clergy.

Still, McMillin's biography is more than the story of a fascinating sport hero held up as an example for young men. It offers a major illustration of the complex way in which football became an integrated component of American society. His career (1912-1952) spanned the most formative period in the development of the game. He played in high school during the years when football first assumed much of its modern form and was rapidly being taken up by secondary schools. His college experience came in the period when this sport dominated the nation's campuses and in the eyes of many threatened the values of higher education. Finally, he made the transition to the National Football League after World War II just as the professional began to overshadow the college game.

Beyond the internal history of football, the life of this unique man raises and illuminates some of the perennial questions about the place of sport in American society: the influence of coaches over their players, athletics as a tool of colleges in attracting students and raising endowments, the connection between sport and religion, society's need for heroes, and the symbiotic relationship of the press to the athletic programs of schools.

As columnist Egan predicted, Bo McMillin lived on in the memories of a multitude of Americans. This biography affords an opportunity for new generations to know this fascinating and significant player, coach, and — above all — human being.

CHAPTER ONE

Redemption Through Football

(1895-1917)

The writer cannot approach this subject [his coaching at North Side Fort Worth High School] without a thrill of pleasure and pardonable pride. It has been his happy lot to have been associated with the young men composing the athletic teams of North Side for several years; to have shared in their many victories and in most of their good times in and out of school as a comrade and friend. He has watched raw boys develop and grow into big and splendid young men through their participation in athletic sports. Not once during these years was his confidence misplaced or his trust violated. There is hardly anything that a bunch of vigorous, red-blooded boys, working together, cannot accomplish in athletics.

Robert L. Myers (1916)

On 28 October 1958, nearly 2,000 former players, coaches, newspaper men, and assorted dignitaries crowded into the Grand Ballroom of New York City's Hotel Astor for the first annual Football Hall of Fame dinner. The climax of the evening came in the presentation of a gold medal to a former West Point football player, now the President of the United States, Dwight D. Eisenhower. When the president rose to speak in response, he apologized for the brevity of his prepared remarks:

> Indeed, so bare did I feel was my cupboard of good subjects for an after-dinner talk, that I am prompted to tell one story, not about football, but about a very great football player and coach when he was a very small boy. The hero — or villain — was Bo McMillin. Bo grew up in a tiny Texas town,...One

Sunday morning the town constable, walking down the street, saw Bo standing in front of the village jewelry store, and strangely he had a very large brick in his hand. He stood there at least ten minutes, and suddenly he threw the brick right through the plate glass window. Stunned, the constable asked Bo how...[he] could ever do such a thing. "Well," Bo said, "you see I'm Catholic — and today I'm on my way to confession. And my trouble, Sir, is that I'm just a mite short of material."

This story was one of the many apocryphal tales McMillin delighted in telling about his early life. Eisenhower knew his audience. No one at this banquet was likely to have missed the significance of the president's reference to McMillin's youth. Followers of football in Eisenhower's generation readily accepted the legend that Bo McMillin's rise to gridiron greatness had begun when a dedicated football coach rescued him from poverty and juvenile delinquency. This theme of the redeeming power of football was dear to the defenders of the large place that this sport occupied in American society. As a coach and spokesman for the game, the mature McMillin found anecdotes from his youth so didactic and entertaining that he embroidered the facts of his early years with a myth partly of his own making. Yet, in this period, as elsewhere throughout his life, the legend had a solid basis in reality.

Alvin Nugent McMillin was born on 12 January 1895, in the rural hamlet of Prairie Hill, in Limestone County, seventeen miles east of Waco, Texas. Apparently no one bothered to — or was required to — file his birth certificate. McMillin was always wary of questions concerning his age, a circumspection that seems to have sprung from a natural reluctance to acknowledge that he had played high school and college football while several years older than most of his teammates. When once in later life he was asked directly by the wife of a faculty colleague about discrepancies in listing his age, he is reported to have replied, "Well, Ma'm, do you want my college age, my playin' age or my courtin' age?"

His sister and the 1900 United States Census agree on the 1895 date, although his military record gives the year as 1896. Some biographical sketches and obituaries, including *Who's Who*, list 1899, apparently on the assumption that he entered college at the usual age. But the family and census records leave little doubt that 1895 was the year of his birth.

The history of his family has been mostly lost in the Irish diaspora to America. Though the Irish had been in Texas almost from the beginning of the American settlement there, the McMillins were too busy making a living in this new land to preserve records of their roots. The younger children knew only one grandparent, Patrick Riley, who lived with the family in his old age. This grandfather had been born in Ireland in 1818 and by 1856 had made his way to Mississippi, where his wife that year gave birth to a daughter, Matilda. By age twenty-three, Maltilda had married Reuben Thomas McMillin, a Texas farmer, and begun bearing children, of whom Alvin Nugent was the seventh of the living. He was two when the family moved to Waco in 1897.

In addition to raising her eight surviving children, Matilda (Mattie to her family and friends) had assumed the responsibility for three of her dead sister's. While living with the McMillins, one of these cousins began calling five year-old Alvin "Bo." The name was soon fixed on the lad, and he became "Bo" for the remainder of his life. Later he seemed to prefer the nickname of "Nuge" from his middle name. But no matter, he became "Bo" to everyone, and even his close friends often never knew or had forgotten his given name.

After four years as a proprietor of a feed store in Waco, Reuben McMillin moved to the flourishing city of Fort Worth, where he found a position with Swift and Company. He eventually settled his large family on the north side of town in a three-bedroom house a few blocks from the stockyards.

Cotton, cattle, hogs, railroads, and more recently oil had made Fort Worth the most prosperous city in Texas. Its population would reach 85,000 during Bo McMillin's fifteen years there. Despite its urban environment, Fort Worth still saw frequent outbreaks of typhoid, malaria, and even hookworm. With nearly 100 churches, Methodists and Baptists dominating, the city presented a strong evangelical face to the world. Revival meetings made headlines and news of the "Sunday School Army" filled columns in the newspapers. Some 8,000 Catholics were barely noticed amid the outburst of Protestant religiosity. Behind this facade of piety two-thirds of the population seldom if ever entered a church. For them, not the church, but pool hall and saloon, baseball diamond and basketball court, sports page and dime novel, brought relief from the drudgery of hard labor. In this thriving city with all of its temptations, Reuben and Mattie McMillin hoped to better the family's lot and, with the help of the Catholic Church, to bring up their children to be God-fearing, responsible adults.

The family was Catholic, but Catholicism in Fort Worth reflected the tone of its evangelical neighbors. At Saint Patrick's Cathedral, which the McMillins attended at first, the sermon topics announced by the pastor in the newspapers were almost indistinguishable from those of local Methodist preachers. The churches, whatever their faith, united in the common mission of teaching the principles of morality on which Christian civilization depended. After moving to the North Side, the McMillins switched to All Saints Church, nearer their home. Mother Mattie made certain that her youngest son was in church each Sunday. In Mass and confession the young Catholic learned the same truth heard from Protestant pulpits: morality was not only essential to society, it richly rewarded the individual who observed its precepts.

Bo McMillin seems to have begun school later than most children, perhaps as a result of the family's moving three times in seven years. Texas had no compulsory school legislation until 1915, and then attendance was required only between ages eight and fourteen. Whenever he began, he became a problem pupil. One of his teachers, Miss Laura Bishop, attempted to teach him water coloring in an early grade:

> The first lesson in drawing in those days was to teach the class how to draw a blue sky. Bo always lost his brush; I carried an extra brush to that building every Tuesday and Thursday and forced it on him. He sat dogged, with just a little twinkle in his eye when he looked up to get my approval of the long dirty streak of deep blue. Then he dropped his brush. Bo was not Caesar's angel then to any teacher.

Bo confronted Miss Bishop again in the upper grades. She spanked him for misbehaving and repeatedly kept him after school for sleeping in class. This Irish lad who hated school and said that he wanted to become a boxer became insufferable to other teachers as well and was suspended indefinitely from school. After a year he came back and asked to be put in Miss Bishop's room. She welcomed him and organized a basketball team, the school's first athletic activity, as an outlet for his energy. But Bo's rough play quickly brought tears to the eyes of his smaller classmates.

In 1910, however, McMillin's interest in school picked up. North Side, the high school he would attend, organized its first football team that September, and brother Reuben quickly became its fullback. Next fall, when Bo entered the ninth grade, he would be eligible for the team. Yet the 1911 season brought only tragedy when typhoid fever struck Bo and his father. Typhoid was still a major killer in the United States, the fifth highest cause of death. With its inadequate sewers, untested water supply, fresh milk, and swarms of flies, Fort Worth was especially fertile ground for the typhoid bacilli. The son survived, though he missed the entire year of school. But the father, now fifty-six and displaying the enervating effects of a life of hard work, slipped into pneumonia and died on 30 November 1911.

In later years Bo McMillin often told stories of his Fort Worth youth as he taught others the lessons he had learned. By so doing he helped to fix the legend that he had come from an impoverished family in which, after his father's death, he had to be the breadwinner and thus was forced to leave school and go to work. Undoubtedly he did work part-time after classes to provide spending money and pay for his school books; and in the summer teenagers could sometimes find temporary work in the stockyards.

Nonetheless, his younger sister Katherine insists that Bo never had to drop out of school for economic reasons. And she recalls no such hardships as the legend suggests. Instead, she remembers that some of the older children were already on their own in 1911, and that three of the daughters living at home were employed, two of them school teachers, whose salaries of seventy to ninety dollars a month provided an adequate subsistence. Mina, the oldest of these three, joined her mother in determining to hold the family together. As the mother aged, Mina increasingly watched over the children at home. Brother Reuben, four years older than Bo, completed high school in the spring of 1912 and was ready to help also. He appears to have paid a higher price than Bo for their father's death because he postponed attending college until 1916. This was a proud, self-sufficient family. Mattie McMillin wanted her children to finish school, and Mina was there to see that they did.

Likewise, the legend of McMillin's juvenile delinquency contains a considerable quantity of hyperbole. Makers of the legend, including Bo himself, pictured the North Side of Fort Worth as a breeding ground for youthful vice. This section of the city mixed industries with the homes of workingmen from a variety of ethnic origins. North Main Street, two blocks from the McMillin home, presented temptations for those with money to spend and those seeking it. Establishments such as the White Rat Pool Hall catered to men from the nearby stockyards, other laborers, and some who found easier ways to make a living. Gambling had become a way of life for many Texans. In this neighborhood Bo was never far from a crap game or a pool table. In his teens he mastered the use of "galloping dominoes" and a cue stick by challenging the town's best. To those who knew him well, these skills would become as fabulous as his deeds on the gridiron. Miss Bishop might have suffered shock had she known the nature of the nighttime "work" that left Bo sleepy in class.

Yet, as far as the record shows, the early delinquency of Bo McMillin, aside from gambling, consisted largely of typical boyish pranks. He ran with such "delinquents" as the Minton brothers: Sherman, the future associate justice of the United States Supreme Court, and the younger Rosco. Following the death of their mother in Indiana, the boys' father had moved to Texas, where Rosco joined him. Although Sherman remained in Indiana for schooling, he spent considerable time in Fort Worth, and both became close to Bo. After McMillin's rise to football fame, the Minton brothers passed on to their children the story of the three young pals stealing a ham one Friday while on a camping trip. When they went to eat it, however, Bo insisted on saving it for the next day because Catholics were forbidden to eat meat on Friday.

This story of mischief within the restrictions of a conscience seems to characterize Bo McMillin's fabled wild oats. As much as he might frequent pool halls and search for crap games, and as good as he was with his fists, he emerged from his Fort Worth years a model young man in many respects. He did not smoke, drink, or swear and was true to his one and only girlfriend. Ignoring the less dramatic and seldom demonstrable influence of his parents, siblings, and priests, the legend attributes his "redemption" to a football coach who snatched him from a life of poverty and delinquency, inculcated high moral standards in him, and set him on the road to future greatness. It was an account embraced in full confidence by sports writers and coaches, and even by parents who hoped that football would have the same influence on their rowdy sons.

By the time Bo entered the ninth grade in 1912, the game of football had become an American passion second only to that of baseball. In the thirty-five years after the Civil War this sport had evolved from soccer into a game more like English rugby, and by 1900 had assumed much of its modern form. Football fever infected college students who thrilled in the contests with rival schools. The alumni swelled with pride in alma mater with each gridiron victory. Newspaper editors and their sports reporters eagerly covered the Saturday contests as a way of increasing circulation. College presidents, especially those of new or obscure institutions, quickly caught on to the value of the publicity generated by a winning team in attracting students and donations to their schools. The advent of the professional coach at the turn of the century marked the institutionalization of college football. So highly did President Theodore Roosevelt value the physical and moral aspects of gridiron combat that he called a White House Conference in 1905 to save the game from critics of its brutality. The ethos of early twentieth century America found expression in the quest for victory on the football field.

Although many private academies had played football as early as the colleges, the expense of mounting a team had slowed its introduction into the public high schools. Most high school students in Fort Worth attended Central High. But the city was required to maintain a small high school on the North Side by terms of the agreement that had annexed that section. North Side High had no football team until Robert Lee Myers arrived there in 1910 to teach physics and chemistry. He at once decided to coach a team, seemingly in compensation for his own frustration as a player. In his undergraduate days at Centre College in Danville, Kentucky, from 1903 to 1906, he had been class poet, editor of the yearbook, an actor in the dramatics club, and was acknowledged to be the "brightest man in college." But his success ended when he put on a football uniform. A small but spirited player, he was dropped from the Centre reserve team after his freshman year, and had to content himself with being manager of the second team the next season. Yet this disappointment only increased his passion for the game. After graduation he worked with his father's Chautauqua company until taking the teaching position at Fort Worth, where he hoped to achieve as a coach the success denied him as a player.

Well liked by his players and students, Myers was dubbed "Chief," an affectionate contrast with Chief Meyers (John Tortes Meyers), the large, hard hitting Indian catcher of the New York Giants. He attempted to improve his knowledge of football by visiting Glen S. "Pop" Warner, one of the first professional coaches, now at the Carlisle Indian School. The scholarly Chief Myers, impeccably dressed in his three piece suit and fedora hat, set out to teach the complicated system of Pop Warner to the handful of boys who turned out for football at North Side. Having "loved and studied foot-ball all his life," he now believed that he could "train his teams in modern scientific football attack and defense, such as is given to older men in the larger colleges and universities."

Bo McMillin's first association with Chief Myers is forever lost in legend. One version, repeated in several obituaries, emphasized the lad's sacrifice for his family: "Bo quit school in Texas when he was 12 years old to support his family and so that his older brother might play football. One day he substituted for a missing player. That was the beginning." More dramatic are the versions of Bo being grabbed by a policeman as he attempted to climb the fence of the Fort Worth professional baseball park. Depending on the account, either Myers saved the boy from arrest by buying him a ticket, or watched in such admiration at Bo's speed in jumping out of the patrol car and running home that he offered him a place on the team. *First Down Kentucky,* the novel for boys based on McMillin's early life, goes even further. Before his future football coach intervened, Bo was successfully fighting off three policemen at once while out of the corner of his eye still watching a football game for which he did not have the price of admission.

However his introduction to Coach Myers, once McMillin went out for football, he for the first time had a motivation to study. He must pass three of his four courses to remain eligible. His high school transcript has not been preserved, so nothing is known about his grades except that Myers made a point of holding to the rules and wanted his players to prepare for college. Miss Bishop, who now took a strong interest in athletics, recorded one instance of Bo's struggle with a difficult subject:

In the freshman year Bo was having the athlete's trouble in making grades. We "checked" the boys closely — and there were no substitutes. On one examination Bo and half the team were struggling with a physics test. They wrote all morning, on till two o'clock. Bo asked for a sandwich. I sent his comrade, who stood in the hall looking in sympathetically. I knew the sandwich would be "loaded." I watched, but no "help" passed. Bo looked steadily at me and began to cram down on the sandwich. Bo failed! He came to my room at four, tears in his eyes, swearing he never had such a rough deal. He had eaten the precious paper that lay next the ham in the sandwich.

The legend of Bo McMillin has centered on the giant killer theme of a small unknown college defeating mighty Harvard in 1921. But McMillin first assumed the giant killer role at North Side High School. Central, the other public high school, had four times as many students and forty or more boys trying to make the squad. In the seasons of 1912 through 1914, Coach Myers had hardly sufficient players to field a team, and never enough for a scrimmage between the first and second teams. North Side seldom played a game in which it was not heavily outweighed by its opponent. "Boys," Chief Myers told his team at the beginning of a season, "play with the theory that there isn't a football eleven in the state that can beat us, ... When you go against a team that outweighs you, don't worry. Use your brains. Where brawn and bulk are lacking, brains will turn the trick." He devised training methods to compensate for his lack of material. For instance he placed all the linemen in a row a few yards apart and required the backs to zigzag in and out of the line to see how many tackles they could break. One observer noticed that McMillin frequently got as far as the sixth tackler in the line. With substitutions permitted only at the beginning of a quarter, Myers knew that nearly all of his men must play the entire game. Thus he demanded a level of physical conditioning rare in high school coaches of this period.

It was a fortunate time for McMillin to enter football. Seventeen in 1912, he had reached his full height of over five feet nine inches and weighed 165 pounds. He was fast but not the fastest, strong but not the strongest. His speed and powerful legs, combined with an amazing agility, ideally suited him for the game that football had become by

1912. Changes in the rules that year resulted in a sport placing more emphasis on speed and deception and less on brute force. The field was given its modern dimensions including end zones, and a forward pass completed in the end zone could now be a touchdown. Passing was permitted from anywhere behind the line of scrimmage, and the ball was made slimmer and thus easier to pass.

High school football in Fort Worth had not yet been highly organized. Coaches served voluntarily and schedules were seldom arranged more than two or three weeks ahead. The two public schools competed with Bryant, a small private boys school, and the academy of Polytechnic College for a silver trophy. YMCA teams were also available for high school games. More important, the newspapers pushed the concept of a state championship in which the best team of North Texas would meet the champion of South Texas. A committee at the University of Texas sought to arrange such a contest and to produce agreement on eligibility rules, but its decisions met with more derision than acceptance. With game officials lacking training and authority, it was not uncommon for teams simply to quit the field and forfeit the game in protest of a disputed call. The quantity of newspaper publicity given to high school football belied the haphazard nature of the contests.

Ideally such a legendary player as Bo McMillin should have enjoyed gridiron success from the beginning. But it required two agonizing seasons for Chief Myers to hone the young man's rich talent. He placed Bo at left halfback, from which position he could run the tricky Carlisle plays, and he would stay there for four years even though he was soon calling signals instead of the quarterback. It was apparent from almost the beginning that McMillin was the team's natural leader.

In the 1912 season North Side was heavily outweighed in nearly every game and had only two substitutes. Nonetheless, the team managed to win two games and tie one. In the contests with major rivals, however, North Side found itself exhausted before the last quarter and helplessly watched its goal line crossed repeatedly. Most humiliating of all, Central beat North Side for the city championship 60-0. The undefeated Central team, unscored on by any opponent, now claimed the state championship. One writer placed part of the blame for North Side's failure on the coach's using plays too complicated for his inexperienced team to execute. If Chief Myers could take any consolation from this disastrous season, it may have been that Bo McMillin had shown occasional flashes of brilliant running ability. His dodging and stiff-arming already drew much attention from fans and reporters.

With eighteen on the squad in 1913, the North Side team began to show promise. It made headlines when McMillin ran for a touchdown in a practice game against Polytechnic College, a Fort Worth school that would play the University of Texas the next weekend. Then North Side rolled up large scores against two opponents before barely defeating its local rival, Bryant. In that game the team suffered a crippling blow when James R. "Red" Weaver fractured his wrist. Playing center at only 160 pounds, Weaver had become the mainstay of the line. With Weaver gone for the season, North Side lost any hope of winning the state championship when it was defeated 6-0 by Comanche, one of the contenders.

Chief Myers testified to his standards during the 1913 season by refusing to play Central unless two players he considered ineligible were removed from that team. One had been on a college team the previous year, and the other had played professional baseball during the summer. Central, so powerful in 1913 that it defeated Texas Christian University 26-0, refused to drop the two. Myers's complaint was instrumental in having Central declared ineligible for the state championship, The resulting controversy reached the point that the Central principal had to suspend the entire team from athletics for a year for verbally abusing some of their teachers who objected to the emphasis on football. Myers had won his case. In February 1914 the eligibility rules for the entire state were strengthened.

By now Bo McMillin at nineteen was entirely consumed by a love of sport. After football came basketball, a game invented in 1891 to provide indoor recreation during the winter. But the "stockyards team," as North Side was known, had no gymnasium and played its home games on an outside court. Bo and a half dozen of his football teammates seemed at first to play basketball as roughly as they had blocked on the gridiron, and achieved little initial success. Yet by Bo's final season at North Side (winter of 1915-1916), his team went through the state tournament easily to win the Texas championship. As in football, he was the playmaker. After one game a writer commented of

McMillin that "hardly a play was started or a basket made that he did not directly or indirectly figure in landing it."

Basketball initially provided a better outlet for the talents of William Madison (Matty) Bell, a slender six-footer and excellent student who was too awkward and slow to become a football regular until his senior year. By following his coach's regimen, Bell developed into a capable athlete who would play college football with Bo and go on to a distinguished coaching career. Here again Chief Myers witnessed the redemptive power of sport as a bright but physically inept boy was turned into a man who excelled with his body as well as with his mind.

McMillin turned to the spring sports with equal enthusiasm. He quickly discovered that his best position in baseball was at second base, where his agility enabled him to make sensational plays. In one high school track meet he was sufficiently versatile to place second in three events: the pole vault, shotput, and 440 yard race. In these sports, as in football, the combination of his natural endowment and acquired determination produced an athlete of uncommon aptitude.

Still, football remained his greatest passion. After the World Series in early October, the sport pages of the *Fort Worth Star-Telegram* were filled with little else but details of college football in every section of the nation. Readers followed the triumphs of Harvard's great teams as eagerly as they hoped that Coach Charlie Moran could produce a winner at Texas A & M. Walter Camp's annual All-American selections were awaited with anticipation and often greeted with controversy by those who believed that their favorite players had been slighted. A vast outpouring of football fiction, much of it aimed at boys, kept alive in the hearts of high school players the dream that someday they too could star for a college team. Much of this literature was didactic. It taught the importance of school spirit, teamwork, and moral commitment. Athletics could turn any boy willing to work hard into a man and prepare him to meet the challenges of adult life. At North Side High School Chief Myers preached this gospel of football to eager converts, none more receptive than his star halfback.

The 1914 season began with a practice game against Texas Christian University in which, although the college team won, Captain McMillin bucked through center for a touchdown. Then the "stockyards team" rolled up large scores against several opponents — one 80-0 — and went on to defeat all its North Texas rivals. The team had at last mastered the plays taught by Myers, many of which called for Bo to throw a forward pass. "At left half," proclaimed a reporter, "is the peer of all Texas high school players, 'Bo' McMillin. He is a team within himself. On defense he is in nearly every play. On offense he is a terror. His forward passing rivals that of...college stars."

The two overpowering Texas high school football teams met in the state championship game of 1914. Thus far in the season, Austin had scored 232 points to its opponents' 9, and North Side 250 to 14. The Fort Worth boys refused to be daunted by Austin's fielding three teams, all appearing to be equally heavy. After a scoreless first half, Austin took advantage of fumbles by the North Side team to win 23-0. Nevertheless, it had been a glorious season for the little school from the stockyards district. Coach Myers had brought his team this far while holding to the eligibility rules.

The influence of coach, family, church, and teachers had clearly left its mark on this Irish halfback. At the end of the 1914-1915 school year, he wrote to Miss Bishop, now his English teacher, a letter which she preserved and long cherished:

> Dear Miss Bishop:
>
> You know sometimes when a fellow gets the blues, and he has the idea the whole world is down on him — when he is only down on himself — that a smile on the face of someone he likes certainly does help a lot; I want to say here that I thank you for the smile that I have seen so often on your lips. I also want to thank you in behalf of the fellows, Mr. Myers, and myself for the never dying loyalty you showed all thru the year.... You certainly did win a warm place in the hearts of us football boys last fall by your loyal support; and I want to say too, for myself that you have made school life a pleasure instead of a drag as it has been in years past.
>
> I consider it a great pleasure to say that I am one of Miss Bishop's pupils.
>
> Your loving pupil,
>
> Bo McMillin

In this letter he already had begun to display the sly Irish blarney clothed in a Texas drawl with which in later years he would charm and amuse audiences throughout the nation.

The 1915 season duplicated the last. With eight regulars back, North Side aimed for the state championship. Sherman "Shay" Minton, who had played football at Indiana University, was in town long enough to teach the squad some of his college plays. Although McMillin had contracted malaria during the summer and lost nearly fifteen pounds, he seemed faster than ever. All went as expected, and last year's teams met again in the state championship game. Austin scored in the first quarter, after which North Side played a determined defensive game but could not cross the goal line of the heavier team. McMillin's passes went mostly for incompletions because his ends could not get into the clear, and the game ended 6-0. The disappointment of losing the state championship by a single touchdown was partially alleviated when North Side defeated Central 47-0, thus avenging the humiliating loss of 1912 to the local rival.

One game in 1915 brought to the surface the quality of McMillin's leadership on the field. In a fierce contest against Waxahachie, the referee penalized North Side for both holding and being offside on a single play. When Bo vehemently demanded to see where in the rulebook it was permitted to impose two penalties on one play, he was ejected from the game. In the last period with the score 14-0 against his team, Myers — apparently with urging from Bo on the sidelines — decided that the local official had been part of a plot by Waxahachie to "get McMillin out of the game and we will win." Chief then refused to continue unless Bo was allowed to return. The referee remained adamant, and North Side forfeited the game. From this and other examples, football reporters concluded that the "brainy" left halfback who called signals, ran, passed, and punted, who amazed the spectators with his "wonderful sidestepping," was also the "think tank of the North Siders" and the on-the-field "boss." Chief Myers regarded himself as a teacher of football, not a field general; thus he was happy to let such a natural leader as McMillin exercise considerable control once the game began.

It had been a bruising, emotional season for the North Siders. In one game on a scorching day McMillin had been so overcome by heat that

— in the absence of locker room facilities — his teammates revived him at halftime by throwing him into a nearby lake. Bo was often singled out by opposing teams for physical abuse, a practice that only increased the intensity with which he and the team played. Myers wrote of this season, "We were known as a crying team. We cried when we lost and we cried when we won. When a man would be hurt, the others would cry over him and bind up his hurts and call him brother, and then all go in and play a game that was a thing of glory. And the Coach would cry with them, for he, too, was their brother."

Myers left the high school in June 1916 to assist in his father's Chautauqua business. He urged his graduating players to go on to college, and he hoped that he could recruit the best of them for his alma mater, Centre College in Danville, Kentucky. McMillin never forgot the "word pictures" Myers painted of Centre while urging his players to try for greatness:

> Himself a graduate of Centre, he told us he hoped to go back there some day as coach and that we would go with him....He pictured the great record we could make in football, if we would do our class work and make the sacrifices that he asked of us for the good of ourselves, as well as for football. He said,... "Bo, you'll be the All-American Quarterback; and Red Weaver, you'll make All-American Center; and in spite of your size, Matty Bell, you'll be one of America's greatest ends."

Matty Bell responded to his mentor's advice and took his excellent academic record to Centre. With him went teammate Bob "Hunk" Mathias, and several other players resolved to come after graduation in a year or two. But Rosco "Cow" Minton, who had played all four years with Bo, enrolled instead at Indiana University.

Above all, Myers wanted Bo on the Danville campus. Under the new four-year rule, Bo could not play another season at North Side or any Texas high school. Yet he was several credits short of the required fourteen high school units that Centre and other colleges with high academic standards required for even conditional admission.

Myers, apparently with considerable help from the president of Centre, arranged for McMillin to play at Somerset High School, located in a small town in the mountains forty miles south of Danville. A self-appointed committee of local citizens had determined to give the town a winning team that would boost civic pride and provide an opportunity to recover some of the wagers lost to supporters of Kentucky towns whose teams had regularly beaten the Somerset eleven in past years. Calling themselves the "stovepipe committee" because they met around a pot-bellied stove with a long pipe, they had persuaded a college coach, Paul Dexheimer, to locate in their town and direct the team. The Somerset team had gone undefeated in 1915, but the boosters hungered for more and were naturally interested in McMillin.

From Myers's viewpoint, it was a perfect solution. Reuben McMillin, who would enter Centre in the fall of 1916, would be near enough to keep a watchful eye on his younger brother, safely removed from the stockyards environment. And Bo would have an additional year of playing experience under an excellent coach while he completed high school.

The "stove-pipe committee" also took under its wing Red Weaver, who gave up the captaincy of the North Side team for 1916 in order to follow Bo to Somerset. To support the two, thirty Somerset gentlemen agreed to have one suit a month pressed by the boys at a dollar a suit. After the Texans scorched a few suits with what Bo called an "iorn," the business dropped off but the dollars kept coming. And Bo supplemented his "scholarship" at the local pool hall and in crap games against workingmen unaware of this high schooler's reputation as a "shark." The committee also found a motherly lady with whom the boys could live and a football-loving telephone operator who relieved Bo's homesickness by giving him free late night calls to his girlfriend in Fort Worth.

McMillin and Weaver discovered that the Somerset team already had a few capable players, the best of whom was the powerfully built James B. "Red" Roberts. He was Bo's equal at the pool table and an inveterate practical joker. These three, who in college would be named to Walter Camp's All American team, formed the nucleus of a formidable squad that would nearly achieve the goal of the "stovepipe committee." In the first five games of 1916, the Somerset "Mountaineers" crushed their opponents by scoring 301 points while giving up only a single touchdown. But not until the game with Louisville Boys High School did news of this team's strength spread throughout Kentucky. Louisville had scheduled this small-town school as a "breather." After Somerset received the kickoff, the tackle lining up against Roberts contemptuously growled, "Now show me that McMillin the papers have been writing about!" On the first play, Red knocked his large opponent down and said, "Buddy, I am going to let you up in a minute, and if you'll look toward the goal line, you'll see McMillin. He's crossing it with the ball." With Weaver and Roberts at the tackles and McMillin calling signals and running for four touchdowns, Somerset defeated the big-city eleven, 51-0. The next morning, headlines and photographs in the *Louisville Courier-Journal* told of Bo McMillin, "hero" of the contest and the best open-field runner ever seen in the local stadium.

Only the Lexington High team stood between Somerset and the unofficial state championship. Since Lexington had done no better than a tie against Louisville, the 500 "Mountaineer" fans who rode the special train to the game confidently awaited the expected slaughter. They offered odds as high as four to one or even money and twenty-one points. Before 3,000 spectators, an inspired Lexington eleven, though badly outplayed, refused to let its goal line be crossed. A scoreless tie left both schools claiming the championship and the Lexington rooters considerably richer.

McMillin, Weaver, and Roberts also helped to give Somerset a powerful basketball team. Although the "Mountaineers" lost in the final game of the state championship tournament, Bo's outstanding play kept his name on the sports pages.

Still one-half credit short of graduation from high school, McMillin was granted a conditional admission to Centre College in the fall of 1917. Sometime in the months before, he had visited the campus of Indiana University to see his dear friend, "Cow" Minton, who urged Bo to play with him at this Big Ten university. He may have been tempted, and a Louisville newspaper once announced his intention of enrolling at Indiana. There was, however, no appeal in Bloomington as strong as his loyalty to Chief Myers.

If McMillin had not been as "lost" to poverty and delinquency as the legend of his youth would have it, he had still come far from the days when Miss Bishop had tried unsuccessfully to get him to paint the sky blue. His mother, who had faithfully kept him under the influence of the Church, could take a share of the credit for his being in college rather than earning his living in the stockyards or at the gaming tables.

Mina and Reuben had also provided a stabilizing influence. Nevertheless the "redemption" of Bo McMillin owed much to a football player *manqué* from Centre College who took a teaching position in Fort Worth and decided to coach the sport he could not play. When in later years Coach McMillin preached the character-building value of football, he spoke with the conviction of his own experience. "I'm a man who was made by football," he declared to all who would listen; "that's why I owe so much to the game."

CHAPTER TWO

The Praying Colonels
(1917-1919)

*We pray before each football game, for we believe the Lord
sends us the help we ask Him for. . . . Since we began praying before the games we haven't had a man seriously hurt
and it helps to keep the game clean.*

Bo McMillin

Alvin Nugent McMillin was twenty-two when in September
1917 he first settled his lean but muscular frame into a seat in Centre
College's classroom building. He had entered a college noted for high
academic standards and successful graduates. Chartered in 1819 to
train Presbyterian ministers for the region, Centre had soon evolved
into a denominational school "conducted upon liberal, free and enlightened principles," and open to students of any faith as long as they
took the required Bible courses and attended chapel services. While
the Baptists and Methodists won the most converts in Kentucky, the
Presbyterians educated the state's leaders at Centre and the even older
college of that denomination, Transylvania at Lexington. Centre
proudly published a long list of distinguished alumni: two vice presidents of the United States in addition to governors, senators, congress-
men, judges, diplomats, and college presidents, to say nothing of
some hundreds of preachers, lawyers, and physicians. Even Woo-
drow Wilson, while president of Princeton University, had admitted
that "there is a little college down in Kentucky which in sixty years has
graduated more men who have acquired prominence and fame than
has Princeton in her 150 years." These words became especially dear
to Centre men when their author moved into the White House in 1913.

Centre also boasted that it was not coeducational and consequently enjoyed the advantages of fitting men for the "duties and work of life" without the distraction of females. In addition to fielding athletic teams, Centre men staged plays, sent out intercollegiate debate teams, competed for the Latin prize, declaimed in oratorical contests, edited a newspaper and a yearbook, argued in mock trials, and held an annual carnival that climaxed the commencement season. If women were needed for dances or cheerleading, the Kentucky College for Women was conveniently nearby in Danville. Centre permitted fraternities, but there were no houses for the Greeks. Most students had to find quarters in the town, for only seventy could be housed on campus.

Although Bo McMillin pledged to Beta Theta Pi and was elected vice president of the freshman class, he had come to college to play football, not to take advantage of the opportunities for social and intellectual growth provided by this well-rounded educational program. The women he loved — his mother, sisters and girlfriend Marie Miers — were all in Fort Worth. After growing up in that city's evangelical society, he could easily tolerate Centre's Protestantism, but Danville's one Catholic church became his spiritual home while in college. If he had to study, he would when absolutely necessary to remain eligible. In this age before athletic scholarships — and Centre publicly denied that it provided any — he would have to hustle to raise his yearly college expenses of some $300, a necessity, so his classmates maintained, that he met by using cue and dice to extract dollars from the pockets of Danville workingmen. The football players who had come to Centre with him from North Side and Somerset were not always the best influence on him. Yet, whatever McMillin's expectations in September 1917, this little Kentucky college proved to be the ideal institution in which to perfect those heroic qualities that Chief Myers had first seen in this Irish son of Texas.

Centre needed Bo McMillin as much as he needed its wholesome and stimulating environment. During the early 1910's the college had suffered dropping enrollments and increasing deficits. To reverse the tide, in 1915 the trustees had brought in a vigorous new president, William A. Ganfield, who began stumping the region preaching the worth of Old Centre. His efforts produced larger freshman classes, but the American entry into World War I in April 1917 took away so many upperclassmen that the enrollment remained near 100. Undaunted, Ganfield continued his recruiting, launched a major campaign to increase the college's endowment, and cooperated with the national government to provide military training on campus. To further these plans, he intended, as the local newspaper aptly phrased his design, that "the athletic department will be kept well to the front."

The gold and white Centre College Colonels had played football against regional schools since 1880 and had produced a number of notable teams before 1912. Since then the lack of success on the gridiron had matched the depressed state of the college in general. The 1916 team, however, bolstered by Matty Bell, Bob Mathias, and Reuben McMillin from Fort Worth, had won or tied every game except for a 68-0 trouncing by the University of Kentucky (then known as Kentucky State). This crushing defeat did not bode well for President Ganfield's campaign. Evidence is lacking to determine the extent of his influence in recruiting a new coach, but he seemed delighted to announce in March 1917 that Robert L. Myers would return to his alma mater to coach football the next season. If Bo had ever wavered between Centre and Indiana University, the news that he could play under the beloved Chief had settled the issue.

In addition to his love of the game and the loyalty of his former Fort Worth players, Myers enjoyed an additional advantage as coach. As part owner of the White-Myers Chautauqua Company, he employed each summer a dozen or more boys as tent men, ticket takers, platform managers, and advance agents for this traveling company that provided a yearly taste of culture for the communities on its circuit. He offered these jobs first to his football players, thus extending his influence over them and helping to keep them in college. McMillin spent several summers, possibly even during high school, with the Chautauqua company, as did his friends, the Minton brothers. Listening over and over to some of the country's best-known orators who mounted the platforms the boys helped to erect provided an education in public speaking that no college could offer. And players who spent their summers together became more like a family than a team. During his college years Bo worked his way up from tent man to advance publicity agent for the Chautauqua company. In this way also, Myers steered the destiny of the Texas boy he had "redeemed" from the fate of a Fort Worth hustler.

Once classes began, it required all the influence Myers could exert to get Bo McMillin to study. He was bright but little interested in anything unrelated to sport. His grades throughout his five years in college would have a familiar pattern of "D's" and low "C's." Either he studied the bare minimum or his professors made some concessions for the star athlete — probably it took both to get him by. A story, long remembered, told of his sleeping behind the coal stove in a Greek class; but when it came his turn to recite, the professor, who liked football, would awaken Bo, assign him some easy lines to translate, stop him before he could make a mistake, and then let him go back to sleep. It seems typical of McMillin's character that his highest grade — a solid "C" — in his freshman year was in Bible. He liked to joke that he took the "ABC curriculum — Athletics, Bible, and Chapel." Yet the Centre faculty did not hesitate to give him failing grades when he dropped below their minimal standards. Fortunately for him, eligibility rules were not yet hard and fast. Everyone soon recognized the innate brilliance he displayed in gridiron generalship and could easily make allowances for someone who had so much to contribute to the college. Each professor knew the players intimately and dealt with them as individuals, not merely as athletes they saw performing once a week. As his later schooling would demonstrate, McMillin was not a "dumb jock" but a student too preoccupied with sport to become a scholar. Furthermore, he soon began to exercise a healthy moral influence on younger students, another role that quickly endeared him to the college authorities.

In a school as small as Centre, football could be integrated into the social, educational, and religious life of the college. Monday's chapel speaker — usually the president but sometimes even the coach or athletic director — often drew moral lessons from Saturday's game. Football was more than a sport; it was preparation for life, both for those who played it and those who watched. It taught teamwork, sportsmanship, courage, clean living, hard work, overcoming obstacles, coolheadedness, and a host of other qualities needed by the successful man. Above all, it demonstrated that it was the quality of one's life that mattered. Myers preached to Centre students that "a man to be a good football player had to have a strong character as well as a body." He drove this point home as he repeated over and over in chapel and locker room Grantland Rice's poem, "Alumnus Football," or "Bill Jones," as it was usually known, until Bo McMillin knew every word. The poetic Bill Jones, "the shining star upon his college team," was expected by his classmates to "buck to glory in the swirl of Life's big game." But not until after many setbacks from such opponents as "Right Tackle Competition," did he finally learn from "wise old coach Experience" that he must "keep on bucking Failure till you've worn the piker out." The poem concluded with the final score of life:

> Keep coming back, and though the
>   world may romp across your spine,
> Let every game's end find you still
>   upon the battling line;
> For when the One Great Scorer comes to
>   mark against your name,
> He writes — not that you won or lost—
>   but how you played the Game.

Rice ended his poem here, but someone — possibly Myers or even Bo McMillin, as a teammate was later told — added several lines to the version recited at Centre:

> Such is Alumnus Football on the white-
>   chalked field of Life;
> You find the bread line hard to buck,
>   while sorrow crowns the strife;
> But in the fight for name and fame
>   among the world-wide clan,
> "There goes the victor" sinks to naught
>   before "There goes a man."

Each entering class received a thorough indoctrination in these ideals and standards of Old Centre, and anyone not in full accord with them was warned "to retire from the company quickly and not wait to be invited out." In the freshman class of 1917, an Irish Catholic boy from Texas warmed to this message and even resolved to study as much as his other interests permitted.

When practice began, Chief Myers found only a handful of veterans from the 1916 squad. Among the missing was Bo's brother Reuben, who had gone to the army. Starting afresh, the coach shifted Matty Bell, who had called signals the year before, to the line to make room for Bo at quarterback. The new team, built around the nucleus of four former North Siders, opened the season in October by scoring 104 points against a weak opponent. Then came a sobering lesson at Greencastle, Indiana, as DePauw scored on a fluke play to win 6-0.

On the trip home, Myers may well have had some doubts about his ability to coach in the college ranks.

In the gloom of this unexpected defeat, Charles B. Moran of Horse Cave, Kentucky, visited the Danville campus. Known to everyone as "Uncle Charlie," Moran had already enjoyed an impressive record in sport. He had played football at the University of Tennessee and with the Massillon (Ohio) professional team. Among several coaching positions, he had compiled a record of thirty-eight wins with only eight losses and four ties at Texas A & M from 1909 to 1914. Those figures demonstrated, he insisted, that southern colleges need not go East to find a capable coach. His athletic career had also included several years as a minor and major league baseball player, and he had recently become a National League umpire. The baseball season over, he had come home to hunt birds and visit his only son, a freshman out for football.

Moran quickly grasped the potential he saw on the Centre practice field. In addition to McMillin and Weaver, he discerned raw talent in several others. When he offered to help coach, Myers not only accepted but made Moran head coach and paid him out of his own small stipend. To step aside like this was agonizing for one who had long dreamed of returning to his alma mater as coach. And his players from Fort Worth protested at first. But in the "spirit of self-sacrifice," his beloved Chief insisted to Bo that "we need a bigger man than I to coach the Centre team and that man is Charlie Moran." Myers became athletic director, a part-time position which left him free to attend to his business interests, although he also helped coach as much as possible.

Uncle Charlie Moran took charge with zeal. His personality became the dominant force behind the team. " 'Moranism,' " one student observed, "is more than a system of winning games, it is mighty near a religion." A martinet, his style contrasted sharply with Myers'. He drilled the team relentlessly until they charged as a unit with each man carrying out his assignment on every play. To play for Moran a boy had to be tough. It became a standing joke among teammates that their new coach substituted freely: whenever a player dropped dead on the field, a substitute would take his place. On the sidelines during a game, Moran put himself vicariously into every play by using his arms and legs to tackle, kick, run, or pass, as his team's situation demanded. His intensity matched his quarterback's.

Bo McMillin never loved Uncle Charlie as he had the Chief, but he admired a coach who "knew the strategy and fundamentals of football from A to Z." Despite his rigorous methods, Moran remained close to his players. He had developed his own system of taping and padding to prevent injuries and worked long hours to repair the team's poor equipment. As Bo later wrote, "Our coaches went to the dressing rooms and worked with the boys. They taped the ankles before the game, dressed the wounds after the game, helped give them a rubdown after practice every day, and even went so far as to put cleats on the shoes and to work on the uniforms. When a coach does this...he knows that things are going to suit him and that his players will be well taken care of and will have the best possible protection against injury."

At the end of October, the reorganized, revitalized Colonels rolled easily over Maryville College. Next Saturday's homecoming game against the University of Kentucky offered an opportunity to avenge the humiliating defeat of last year. Centre alumni rode into Danville on trains (with tickets sold on commission by the college) for what was heralded as the state's most important game of the year and a revival of the fierce rivalry of the last decade. A delegation from Somerset came to cheer the four Centre players who had brought glory to that town's high school team the year before, and Danville's stores shut to let clerks attend. Supporters of the Colonels eagerly covered the several thousand dollars wagered by State's rooters.

For some long forgotten reason, "My Old Kentucky Home" had become a bad luck omen for the State team, so naturally the Centre band blared out the song on key plays. The Colonels almost needed such help, for their backs ran freely except near the goal line. With no score in the third quarter, McMillin threw a touchdown pass to Ed "Mule" Diddle in the end zone and watched in agony as the ball sailed through the receiver's hands. Years later, when Diddle was a prominent basketball coach, he still recalled what his quarterback said to him in the next huddle: "I pass the ball and old Mule drops it. I run the ball, you don't open up. I guess I'll have to kick the danged ball." In desperation on fourth down from the twenty-yard line, Bo attempted to drop kick a field goal, although he had never kicked in competition before. A wobbly ball barely got over the goal posts to win the game 3-

0, but it was a sufficient victory to touch off a joyous celebration in Danville and to launch a parade at Somerset High School.

The Kentucky game began to demonstrate to the press the abundant material McMillin provided for legend building. Not only could he dazzle with his broken field running and dodging tacklers from one side of the field to the other while trying to throw a a forward pass, he was quotable. He talked incessantly in his Texas drawl before, during, and after a game. And once his style became familiar, writers could put seemingly credible words into his mouth. One version of Bo talking audibly to himself before kicking the winning field goal was typical of what was to come throughout his life: " 'These legs of mine,' said he to himself in a cool calm voice, 'have become notorious for running. They ought to be pretty good old legs for kicking too, it seems to me.' " Similarly, the legend would continue to be created.

John Y. Brown, Sr., a substitute player, remembered many years later that it was in the dressing room before the contest with Kentucky that the Colonels first had pre-game prayer. According to Brown, when Chief Myers mentioned in his pep talk that it might be well to request divine help in conducting themselves on the field like gentlemen, fullback Bob "Hunk" Mathias burst out, "Let me lead that damned prayer." Whenever the custom began, by the 1919 season Centre teams would be known nationally as the "Praying Colonels." More often than not, President Ganfield would be in the locker room to initiate the prayer. He almost never missed home or away games and was usually on the sidelines at practices. It was not unusual for teams of church sponsored colleges to have locker room prayers, but Centre's invoking the divinity would take on legendary proportions.

By now, the quarterback, though a freshman and not yet captain, was clearly the leader of the team. Brown recalled seeing Bo drive off the squad a senior teammate he had caught smoking. Some newspaper stories insisted that he enforced the training rules with his fists. Reporters noticed that Bo did not use profanity and would not permit others to do so in his presence. Instead of curses he drove the team by the emphasis he placed on certain words. An end who dropped a pass, or a tackle who missed a blocking assignment, came back to the huddle with a stinging, sarcastic "MARVELOUS" or "WONDERFUL" ringing in his ears. As close to swearing as Bo ever came was his expression, "Well, I'll be a dirty name."

Gambling, however, was a sport and a source of income, not a vice, to McMillin and the Centre players. They considered it perfectly legitimate to bet on their team to win as long as they did not attempt to hold down the score. Often they wagered their last dollar on a game, especially on away games where the locals did not yet know Centre's strength. And students who could not attend road games sometimes made up purses to send with the team. The college authorities preached against gambling and threatened to dismiss those who did, but to no avail. Far more than school pride rested on the outcome of most gridiron contests for this tiny college.

McMillin's reputation as a gambler soared in his early months at Danville. John Y. Brown no doubt exaggerated somewhat when he remembered that "Bo broke every gambler in the Bluegrass Region shooting craps. In fact, it got so that, finally, the only way people would shoot craps with Bo was if he would shake them in a glass, jump them over a string and bounce them against the wall. Most of them weren't too anxious to shoot craps with him even under that system." Brown's picture of this Texan quarterback roaming the railroad yards at night seeking a game with unsuspecting workers fits the general pattern of his first years at Centre. Brown did, however, distinctly recall once when Bo returned to the campus broke after a dice game:

> He came to Breck Hall about midnight, woke me up and awakened some of the other boys, and together we raked up $500 to stake Bo in a return to that game. He went back and when it came his turn with the dice,…he made six straight passes at $500 a pass. Rather than take a chance on the seventh one, he took his $500 loss out of that, quit and came back to the dorm and gave all the boys their money back.

Still, Centre's influence may have curbed McMillin's love of games of chance. After 1918 he appears to have gambled less, perhaps because the college administration offered to defer his charges for tuition, board, and room. (Whatever the arrangement, in 1924 he would complain that after leaving college he had been billed for his expenses while there.) As a coach in later years, his desire to exert a wholesome influence on his players left him shooting pool and craps for money only with adults wealthier than himself.

After the struggle with Kentucky, Centre defeated its remaining four opponents without having its goal line crossed. By the end of the season the excitement generated by this "Grand Team" had begun to spread throughout the state. It is, proclaimed Kentucky's leading newspaper, an "eleven full of stars" who nonetheless had exhibited perfect teamwork. Red Weaver, too light to be a center, had played the position like a wild man, even defying his physician by playing in the final game with two broken ribs. Recovered from the knee injury that had left him ineffective in 1916, fullback Bob Mathias had regained the line-smashing form he had shown at North Side. Freshman Norris "Army" Armstrong had proved to be an end of unusual speed and determination. Matty Bell had made a gallant effort to use his string-bean body at tackle before shifting to his more natural position at end. Playing every minute of every game, Bo McMillin had been as notable for his direction of the team as for his own running and passing. After scoring 247 points to their opponents' 6, the Colonels obviously were ready for stiffer competition.

Yet, as the cold, snowy winter of 1917-18 set in, the prospects of the next football season seemed less important than the imminent possibility of military service. The federal government approved the continuation of college athletics for those students still on campuses, but Centre men continued to enlist. At halftime of the first basketball game in January, the crowd cheered not only the playing of McMillin and Bell, but also the announcement that five of their football teammates were going to the army. Bo finished out the basketball season, with his team losing only once and claiming the state championship.

Never one to shy away from a fight, McMillin enlisted in the United States Naval Reserve at Dallas, Texas, on 11 June 1918. The naval surgeon who gave him the required physical examination noted a man of five feet nine inches, 170 pounds, with blue eyes, dark brown hair, a ruddy complexion, and several scars. The new seaman appears not to have reported for active duty until the beginning of September. In the meantime the federal government was undertaking an elaborate plan to use the nation's colleges to train the officers that a protracted war would need. Each college that volunteered would on the first of October become a "little West Point," a unit of the Student Army Training Corps. The government provided pay, subsistence, housing, and uniforms in return for students following a program of military studies and drill. Along with most institutions of higher education, Centre gladly accepted its patriotic obligation. The "Old Centre" building, erected in 1820, was taken over and renovated as headquarters for the SATC. To President Ganfield's surprise and delight, 240 students arrived in Danville for the fall term, most of them eager to remain in college under military discipline at a dollar a day rather than going directly to the army.

Bo McMillin was transferred to the unit at Centre College on 1 October 1918, the day the law creating the SATC went into effect. The question of why one already enlisted in the navy would be sent to a campus unit of the army to play football cannot be answered from the extant records, although the suspicion exists that President Ganfield may have prevailed upon Kentucky's congressional delegation to get Centre's great quarterback returned to the Danville campus.

The Centre campus was a military camp during the fall term of 1918. Early morning drill under an army lieutenant was followed by classes in war issues, navigation, mathematics, and English. "Seaman" McMillin flunked navigation but received an "A" in war issues, the first and last time he would earn above a "C" in his years at Centre. Nonetheless, his participation in the SATC would have important consequences. The Centre faculty and trustees granted to a few seniors whose studies had been interrupted by the war sufficient "war credits" to graduate. This precedent would be unearthed nineteen years later to at last award McMillin his degree. After the armistice in November, the SATC was dissolved in time for the regular academic term to begin in January.

Meanwhile, the Colonels had enjoyed a successful if shortened football season despite the war and a severe flu epidemic in the fall. Red Roberts, Bo's pal from the Somerset team, had entered Centre in September and at once became a source of power wherever he played. Chief Myers had recruited another North Sider, Ralph Montgomery, who at tackle was the largest and strongest man on the squad. These two more than compensated for the loss of Bob Mathias, who had left college. Fearing that McMillin might not be released from the navy, Moran had located another quarterback, Joseph "Chic" Murphy, both the smallest and fastest Colonel.

The war and flu made it impossible to arrange a regular schedule. So severe was the flu in Danville that the team could play no games until 2 November when Transylvania was crushed 44-0. Next Saturday the Great Lakes Naval Training Station brought to Danville a team composed of college players, including such stars as George Halas and Charles Bachman, both soon to gain more fame as coaches. Seeking to get as much income as possible from an abbreviated season, the college offered the innovation of box seats and automobile spaces at Cheek Field. The superior teamwork of the Colonels overcame the heavier sailors, 23-0. The importance of Roberts to his team became clear as he repeatedly tore through the line and once drop kicked a fifty-yard field goal. He was as conspicuous for his appearance as for his play. Refusing to wear a helmet, he taped his ears to his head to prevent their being torn off. The white tape contrasted sharply with his bright red hair and made him conspicuously visible on every play.

Camp Taylor came to Danville on 22 November with an even stronger collection of college players. In a fierce struggle, the Colonels had their goal line crossed for the only time of the season but managed to pass their way to a 10-6 win. The Thanksgiving Day game with Georgetown proved to be no contest. Students celebrated both the end of the war and their fabulous football team. They gloated that Kentucky and Georgia Tech had given, so they believed, lame excuses for not playing the Colonels. Centre, they insisted, had the best team in the South, and they were confident that the next season, in the college's centennial year, would prove it. As certain as the students, President Ganfield announced a new campaign to raise the endowment. From the Danville campus rang the chorus of the college song,

> So come and let us join our voices
> To shout Old Centre's praise,
> Our courage is high, our hearts with faith are strong
> Until the end of days.

Returning to his regular studies in the winter term, McMillin managed to get a low passing grade in four of his five courses. Through the middle of March his time was taken up with basketball. He, Roberts, and Bell were the heart of a team that swept through their eleven games without a loss and with few close contests. Never a polished basketball player, Bo nonetheless brought to the court an intensity and an aggressiveness in fighting for the ball that made him a terror. He played every minute of every game and, more remarkable, never fouled out. Spring brought baseball and track. Again making his spectacular plays at second base, Bo was dubbed "Eddie Collins" by his teammates, a flattering comparison with the great second sacker of the Philadelphia Athletics. In track, he entered several events where his determination partially compensated for his lack of championship speed and strength. Winning letters in four sports only whetted his appetite for future competition.

In September 1919, after a summer of pitching tents for the chautauqua, Bo McMillin impatiently awaited the opening of the football season. The sport had emerged from the war more popular than ever. Only a few voices advocated that the curtailment of the game during 1918 made this a propitious moment in which at long last to correct the evils of football—overemphasis, commercialization, brutality, academic dishonesty — and perhaps even to return the game to its intramural, student directed origin. Most commentators, however, agreed with William W. Roper, Princeton's respected coach, that American football's "value as a developer of manly men has received a complete vindication" on the battlefields of Europe. If there were any critics in Kentucky, their voices were muted by a roaring wave of anticipation coming from followers of the Centre College Colonels. In addition to the traditional rivals, the schedule for 1919 included games with three major teams: Indiana University, the University of Virginia, and West Virginia University.

Myers directed the squad until Moran could be released from his umpiring duties; and now, as captain, McMillin exercised even more authority over his teammates. When a number of promising new players turned out for practice, the Chief announced that all positions were open and that more men would get to play than in the past. As the competition increased, the recruits who did not fold under the rigors of practice gave the Colonels a strengthened squad. Myers provided a training table where all the players ate together. Then when Moran reached Danville he took over with unrelenting rigor. He introduced new plays and perfected old ones. With more first-rate backs, their "positions were often made interchangeable to aid in carrying out plays, and also to bewilder the opponents." In short, as one student commented, Moran put the Colonels through "what Sherman said war was" to prepare them for the big-time teams on the 1919 schedule.

In the first contest, more like track than football, the Colonels ran up a score of 95-0 against Hanover College while starting all plays from punt formation in order not to show their regular formations to the Indiana scouts in the stands. The next Saturday they traveled to

Bloomington to play the heavier Hoosiers. At game time, when Bo went to the center of the field to meet the Indiana captain, he faced his best friend, Rosco Minton. The two captains unashamedly burst into tears at the realization of their being on opposite sides for the first time. In heavy rain on a muddy field, after two Centre touchdowns had been cancelled by penalties, the Hoosiers held a 3-0 lead with less than three minutes to go. Their band was preparing to lead a victory march onto the field when Centre recovered a fumble on the Indiana forty-yard line. On a silent signal, the center snapped the ball to Bo, who shot a surprise pass to Armstrong for sixteen yards. Then in three plunges Roberts went over for a touchdown. In desperation, the Hoosiers tried to come back with a last-minute pass intended for Minton, but Bo intercepted and ran for another touchdown. Despite the 12-3 score, Indiana had been badly outplayed. The Colonels had won, said Myers in Monday's chapel, because "they called upon their inner resources" to overcome the harsh conditions under which the game was played.

A cancelled game for 11 October gave most of the players the opportunity of seeing their intrastate rival Kentucky play Indiana at Louisville. Instead of accompanying his teammates, Bo was sent to Pittsburgh to scout West Virginia against the University of Pittsburgh. He watched the highly-touted West Virginia team fumble away the game in the mud and came home convinced that the Colonels could win against this nationally-ranked opponent they were scheduled to meet on 8 November. Centre's one-sided victories in its two remaining games in October did nothing to shake his confidence.

By now the *Louisville Courier-Journal* had begun to promote Centre College and Bo McMillin. More than a newspaper, the *Courier-Journal* was becoming an all-Kentucky institution that bound the state together with a daily edition soon to be available in every county and home-delivered in most. Once the editors caught on to the appeal of an isolated little college of 200 boys doing gridiron battle with some of the nation's best teams, they spared no effort or expense in telling the story of the Colonels and, as one of the paper's reporters wrote, of " 'Bo' McMillin, the man who made Centre what it is today." Furthermore, Moran had played high school football with and remained a friend of Grantland Rice, whose "Sportlight" column in the *New York Tribune* was widely syndicated throughout the country. Thus as the

Colonels boarded a pullman car for Charlottesville, Virginia, to open their invasion of the East, they needed only continued victories to maintain and even increase the flow of publicity.

Before the game with the University of Virginia, the Centre squad had been strengthened by the addition of Terry Snoddy, a fast end. A high school star, he had played the year before at Kentucky but had now switched to Centre as the result of being refused his letter because the coach thought that he dropped too many passes. Without the rule later adopted that required transferring players to sit out a year, Snoddy could be inserted in the lineup immediately. According to John Y. Brown, Sr., Bo employed near hypnosis on Snoddy to convince him that this quarterback threw passes in such a way that they were almost impossible to drop. Whatever worked the change, "Terrible Teddy" Snoddy proved to be a major addition.

Since Harvard had beaten Virginia 47-0 the week before, Moran wanted to run up a higher score. A muddy field slowed the offense somewhat, but still the Colonels won 49-7, with McMillin gaining 253 yards. For the first time this season, a southern college had defeated a major eastern school. The Danville newspaper trumpeted that Centre was at least now on a par with Harvard, but the students needed no convincing as they welcomed the team home Sunday evening with a snake dance through the town. Some of the players reached their campus with more than pride, if one can believe a University of Virginia professor who complained that a number of Colonels had bet "large sums of money" on their team to win. Bo himself was reported to have bet that he would score more points than the entire Virginia team. He did. While the Colonels ran up the score, a Centre student roamed the stands offering Virginia rooters as much as thirty points.

Yet, outside of Kentucky, Moran's team was not highly regarded. Next weekend the squad, accompanied by a trainload of students and boosters, including the governor-elect of the state, traveled to Charleston to meet West Virginia. The Mountaineer coach thought so little of Centre that he left an assistant in charge while he went to scout a future opponent he considered more difficult. Except for its mud-splattered loss to Pittsburgh, West Virginia had been unscored on this season and was still ranked among the nation's best. The week before it had crushed the Ivy League power Princeton 25-0. As the Princeton game had shown, the Mountaineers' two-hundred pound fullback could hurl the pigskin fifty yards as well as crash through the line for long gains. Much outweighed, the Colonels averaged a mere 170 pounds, and Red Weaver played center at only 155. Delighted to be supporting the underdog, the Kentuckians found West Virginia fans offering odds of two to one, or even money and fourteen points, and eagerly accepted.

As game time neared, Moran finished taping the players, then drew them around him to explain the importance of this day. "Boys," he was reported as saying, "we are about to take the field in the most vital game in the history of Centre College.... This game either makes or breaks us.... You are entrusted this day with the honor of Centre College and Kentucky." By now the team was in tears as President Ganfield prayed for the college and the state. But Bo asked for more prayers and, according to one account, offered one himself before leading his wet-eyed teammates onto the field. Someone overheard the loud praying in the locker room and told reporters. That day the football team from Centre College became the "Praying Colonels" on the sports pages of the nation.

The game began with the Mountaineers looking like an easy winner as they scored in the first five minutes with bewildering power plays. In the second quarter, however, the Colonels stiffened their defense. McMillin tossed a touchdown pass, only to have it called back because he had thrown from fewer than five yards behind the line of scrimmage, as the rule then required. The half ended 6-0. After the intermission, Centre scored on a drive that included a pass from Bo to Bell and a run by Roberts for the touchdown. By now the Colonels were clearly superior; three times they stopped West Virginia inside the ten-yard line. Then in the last quarter McMillin ran for another touchdown to complete a 14-6 victory that thrust Centre into the ranks of the major football colleges of the nation. Football fever swept through Kentucky. "For the first time," proclaimed a Louisville newspaper, "Kentucky is on the football map." Other writers began to suggest that some of the Gold and White players deserved All-American recognition. While Centre was playing West Virginia, Harvard and Princeton had tied. Thus comparative scores suggested that the little college in Danville had a team better than those leading the Ivy League. Eager to see the Colonels in action, Louisville businessmen and fans pressured President Ganfield to move to their city next Saturday's game with the University of Kentucky Wildcats. He refused and instead hastily enlarged the capacity of the college's Cheek Field. All week Kentucky newspapers featured in words and pictures the "Mighty Backfield of Centre Eleven," Bo "the Texas Ranger," "Little" Red Weaver who with braces on both knees had outplayed the heavier All-American Mountaineer center, "Chic" Murphy with his ten-second speed, and other Colonels.

On Saturday Danville's stores, decked in gold and white banners, closed at noon so owners and clerks could join the nearly 8,000 alumni and fans of the two schools who overfilled Cheek Field. The new national prohibition law notwithstanding, there appeared to be in the stands, as a reporter observed, plenty of "red stuff" to help guard against the November chill. Gathered in Danville that day, another newspaper extravagantly proclaimed, was "the flower of Kentucky's manhood and almost irresistible specimens of its womanhood." The game did not live up to its billing, however, as Centre swept over the Wildcats 56-0, despite several of the Colonels still suffering injuries from the West Virginia game. Ignoring his badly bruised ribs, Bo threw a fifty-yard pass for the final touchdown.

After an absence of three weeks on business, Chief Myers had arrived in time to celebrate this victory. The team he had brought together with its five North Side boys as a nucleus was now the pride of all Kentucky and a subject of increasing national interest. He read in the *Danville Daily Messenger* reprints of articles heralding the Colonels from such prestigious sources as the *Washington Post* and the *Harvard Review*. The *Louisville Courier-Journal* pointed out that Ohio State, the Big Ten leader, had beaten Kentucky by eight points fewer than Centre. As Myers had prophesied to his high school players in 1915, gridiron greatness lay before them.

The final games with Depauw and traditional rival Georgetown (KY) were merely showcases for the power of the Centre eleven that finished the season undefeated after scoring 485 points to its opponents' 22. This college of 200 boys had as good a claim as any major university to the mythical national championship. The other contenders — Harvard, Notre Dame, and Texas A & M — had played schedules like Centre's with a mixture of strong and weak teams, and the Colonels had scored 200 points more than any of them, despite having played five of their games in rain and mud. Even after reducing his own total by letting others carry the ball near the goal line, McMillin, with 122 points, was the second highest individual scorer in the country. Whatever doubt might exist elsewhere as to the nation's best team, there was none in Kentucky and least of all in the mind of Bo McMillin.

If his confidence needed further bolstering, it came in the arrival of two easterners to see the last game. Eddie Mahan, Harvard's assistant coach and an All-American of 1915, and Howard Reynolds, a writer for the *Boston Post*, spent several days in Danville scouting the Colonels, looking over the college, and attending a team banquet. Upon their return, they wrote for the *Post* generous assessments of the spirit, teamwork, and ability of the Colonels and particularly of the skill and leadership of McMillin, the captain who enforced the strict training rules with his bare fists. As a result of these articles, Harvard joined the dozens of notable teams seeking a game with Centre for 1920. In December the local newspaper proudly announced that the Colonels had accepted the invitation to play at Cambridge next year.

Further confirmation of Centre's place in the football world came when Walter Camp published his All-American selections in *Colliers'* on 10 December. Although some newspapers and coaches also chose All-American teams, Camp, regarded as "the father of American football," had started the practice in 1889, and his selections had come to be considered almost official. On his first team for 1919 he placed McMillin at quarterback and Weaver at center, with Roberts at end on the third team. Camp had been influenced largely by the performance of these three in the game with West Virginia, although as the most successful promoter of football, he may have foreseen the harvest of publicity to be reaped by bestowing such honors on a small and hitherto unknown college. With these selections, Camp acknowledged that Centre was the strongest football team in the country.

The college newspaper of the University of West Virginia raised the question that must have been on the minds of many followers of football: did Centre play "ringers," especially from Texas, who were not true undergraduate students? Among those rushing to the college's defense was Rosco Minton in a letter to the editor testifying to his knowledge that the North Siders with whom he had played had been high school students who had come to Danville because of the influence of Chief Myers. Centre announced that it would not play West Virginia again without an apology for the outrageous charge. But it would not be the last time anyone would question how such a small college could have three All-Americans.

At the joyous banquets given by alumni for the team in Louisville and Danville, Myers spoke of the importance of prayer before games. The players emphasized teamwork and personal sacrifice for the good of the team. They recalled how Captain McMillin had kept down his own point total by calling the numbers of others when inside the opponents' ten-yard line. More than a team, they were all brothers who loved each other and would fight and if necessary die for their teammates. In this spirit, Bo announced that he would not consider being captain again; it was someone else's turn. When he was reelected despite his protestations, he burst into tears. The only less than euphoric note at the final banquet was struck by President Ganfield's warning to the players against gambling.

After all of this emphasis on team spirit, Moran knew that football fans wanted heroes, not tales of brotherly love. In an article by him in the *New York Tribune* — no doubt arranged by his friend Grantland Rice — he attributed Centre's national championship to one man: "The success of the team has been due largely to Captain Bo McMillin....McMillin can do anything on a football field. And how he can run a team! In a game he is better than two assistant coaches. Always on his toes, he exerts such a powerful influence over the other players that they never give up. The team has great spirit, but it gets most of it from this wonderful youngster. I prefer him to any three players on any team in the country."

The 1919 season had put Centre College and Danville on the map and given the nation a new football hero. Yet, despite Kentucky's pride in the Colonels, Centre's success drew attention as much for its rustic quality as for its record. As a writer for the *Courier-Journal* lamented, "Eastern and Northern papers have pictured Centre College as an institution composed of boys wearing homespun and overalls seeking education in a town cached in deep mountainous valleys. Their pictures of Danville would have the college at the end of the trail of the lonesome pine, listening nightly to the howl of the mountain bobcats and 'varmints' that infest the thickets in the valleys." It was time for Americans to learn that Kentucky's history went back to the American Revolution and that the movement for statehood had begun in Danville even before the adoption of the Federal Constitution! In this way, Centre College had become a symbol of Kentucky pride, but as the next two years would show, it was a symbol that could transcend the boundaries of a state or even a region.

On New Year's Day, McMillin enjoyed a triumphal return to Fort Worth to play in an exhibition game of former high school all-stars. In a contest climaxed by his seventy-five yard run for a touchdown, his squad of North Siders won 21-0. The press praised his heroic fortitude in playing despite having received word that morning of the death of his oldest brother, Evans.

Bo played less basketball that winter, probably because he needed to recover fully from football injuries and to concentrate on his studies. When he did start playing he dislocated a shoulder and had to sit out. And the indoor game may not have been as much fun with his pal Red Weaver unable to play while recovering from a knee operation. Furthermore, Moran returned to Danville for a few weeks before the National League baseball season to institute spring football practice, an innovation for southern colleges.

Commencement 1920 brought the joy of carnival week, but with it a disappointment. The King of the Carnival, William Madison Bell, had resisted all efforts to persuade him to remain at Centre for another football season. He had sufficient credits to graduate, but the nation's colleges had granted another year of eligibility to those who played in the war-shortened 1918 season. Even the lure of a game against Harvard next season failed to lessen Bell's determination to enter law school. He took his Centre sheepskin and left Danville, never dreaming that instead of his intended career at the bar he was headed for distinction as a football coach.

As President Ganfield handed Bell and the sixteen other graduates their diplomas, he could take pride in his administration. Applications for admission for the coming year were the highest in the college's history. Dozens of major football teams wanted to play Centre, so many that even Notre Dame's request for a game had to be turned down. And the trustees had recently raised the goal of their endowment campaign to a million dollars. As a writer in a Louisville newspaper proclaimed, "Kentucky is now noted for its beautiful women, fast horses, and the Centre College football team."

As much as Centre might boast of its distinguished graduates of the past century, it had taken a poor boy from the stockyards of Fort Worth to bring the college to the attention of the nation.

CHAPTER THREE

David and Goliath

(1920-1921)

Centre suddenly became a name to conjure with from Bangor to San Diego, from Duluth to Laredo....For ask the man in Butte, Montana, who are the Senators from Kentucky, and you will get a blank stare for your answer. Ask who is the Governor of Kentucky, and you will know that ignorance can be bliss. But ask the man of Butte who is Centre's quarterback, nay, who is Centre College, itself, and your questions will provoke an enthusiatic reaction and a quick response.

Cincinnati Times-Star

By 1920 Kentucky had begun to feel all the forces that were transforming post-World War I American society. The prosperity of the war years had been followed by an economic depression that lowered wages and sent thousands of southerners North looking for factory jobs, only to face competition from the huge influx of European immigrants. The 1920 federal census showed that Danville, like many other towns of the region, had lost population. The Jazz Era loosened the reins on youth and convinced many of their parents that menaces to morals threatened their children on all sides, particularly those forced to seek employment in the growing cities of the North. Even those young people who remained home could now use the automobile to taste nearby urban pleasures, and the movies made those temptations more enticing. Deep divisions of opinion surfaced over the Red scare, the vote for women, prohibition, immigration restrictions, and the League of Nations. As the Black Sox scandal burst into the headlines, even baseball seemed to have lost its pristine purity.

Such an age of rapid and perplexing change called for heroes who could rise above the contentions and uncertainties of the day and re-confirm the virtues of American democratic society. The heroes who emerged to fill this need came largely from sport: Babe Ruth, Jack Dempsey, Knute Rockne, Red Grange, Bill Tilden, and Bobby Jones, to mention the most famous. Bo McMillin, one of the first heroes of this golden age of sport, did not enjoy the lasting nationwide fame of these. But as he led Centre College into its David and Goliath battles with Harvard College in 1920 and 1921, there were few Americans who had not heard of his feats on the gridiron, and many saw in the simple virtues he exemplified a renewed hope that the nation was still sound at heart. For himself, though, he seemed oblivious to the revolutionary changes around him. As always, he single-mindedly devoted himself to the game he loved.

For McMillin and his teammates, the entire 1920 football season was focused on the game with Harvard College scheduled for Saturday, 23 October. Under its first professional coach, Percy D. Haughton, (1908 to 1916.) Harvard had won the mythical national championship three times and replaced Yale as the nation's most celebrated team. Its battles with traditional Ivy League rivals Yale and Princeton had been reported under banner headlines on the sports pages in all sections of the country. Like other high school players, McMillin had followed in his hometown newspaper stories of the great Crimson team of 1914 with its five All-Americans and of repeated Harvard triumphs over the decade. Haughton had made Harvard Stadium with its more than forty thousand seats the center of the football world. Then, after a war-reduced schedule in 1917 and 1918, the Crimson team of 1919, with new coach Robert Fisher, had scored 229 points to its opponents' 19 and finished the season undefeated, though tied by Princeton.

The prospect of tiny Centre playing mighty Harvard, however, meant far more than merely a clash of strong football teams. Football had originated as a gentlemen's sport played in the elitist colleges of the East by young men from aristocratic families. The "Big Three" of the Ivy League—Harvard, Yale, and Princeton — had dominated the publicity given football. When these three, with their famous coaches, condescended to play non-Eastern schools, it was seemingly to demonstrate to provincials how the game should be played. The Harvard-Yale game at the end of each season became the gridiron classic of the year, heralded in novels and short stories as well as by the alumni and press. Consequently, as western and southern colleges took up football, their players and fans had come to resent the implication that the sport was played best at elitist schools. One indication of such resentment, as a writer for the *New York Times* explained, was the zeal with which the rapid rise of Centre College had been hailed. As the Colonels prepared to do battle with Harvard, they were seen by various writers as the hope of the common man against the elite, the West against the East, rural virtue against urban sophistication — in all these causes, a modern David unafraid of the Cambridge Goliath. Perhaps, commented "Uncle Dudley," the famous editorialist of the *Boston Globe,* the " 'fightin', prayin', cryin' Colonels and their captain" would not turn out to be giant killers after all; but the vestige of childhood romanticism in every adult harbored a hope that they would." Thus, concluded "Uncle Dudley" on the day of the 1920 game, "the feeling which pervades the atmosphere today has applications far wider than football." Most of all, however, Centre College represented the pride of Kentucky and southern manhood.

Within its limited resources, Centre College did all it could to prepare the team for its date in Cambridge. Practice opened on 6 September with Moran present for two days before returning to umpiring. Forty men turned out to vie for one of the twenty-seven new gold and white uniforms with pads especially designed to Moran's specifications. Outstanding among the new men was George Chinn, considered to have been the best high school halfback in Kentucky the past season. Five other recruits survived the preliminary cut, made after Uncle Charlie returned at the end of the month and began drilling the team until dark each afternoon. If there was any doubt as to the mainstay of the squad, it was removed in one practice game where McMillin played one half for the first team and the other for the second team. He scored a touchdown in each half, and the game ended in a 7-7 tie.

In its first three games, Centre scored 241 points without having its own goal line crossed. Moran substituted freely to test his new men, and showed the scouts in the stands only four basic plays. Harvard sent a player from last year's varsity to scout the Colonels against Transylvania on 16 October. McMillin did not play in this game, and thus missed the opportunity to compete again against Albert B. "Happy" Chandler, the Transylvania quarterback who would become his close, lifelong friend. That Saturday, Bo was in Cambridge scouting Harvard as it defeated Williams 38-0. He returned with the Harvard plays precisely diagrammed, but he had obviously lost weight on the trip. The story spread that he had gambled away his expense money and got home by riding the rails with little to eat.

He returned weak and distressed by what he had seen of the Crimson's power and finesse and told the coaches that the game would be "a battle between two systems" in which Centre could win only if its "tricks and passes" could "offset their weight and knowledge of old-style methods." As a result of his trip to Cambridge, followed by over-zealous practice sessions, McMillin had lost twenty pounds by the time the team boarded a train for Cambridge the next Thursday morning.

Meanwhile, Danville and all of Kentucky were agog over the coming contest. "Never in the history of athletics," commented a writer in the *New York Times* about Danville, "has there been a town or city so absolutely dedicated to the one cause of victory as is this town just at present." Boys played the game in advance on street corners by imitating Bo's dodging a half-dozen tacklers and then leaping to heave a long pass over the heads of defensive backs. Arrangements were made to report the game by telegraph and telephone to crowds gathered in front of newspapers offices in Danville and most other Kentucky towns. Prominent citizens gave the team a banquet. The night before the Colonels left for Cambridge, two thousand screaming students and townspeople gathered in front of the courthouse for a pep rally, and a parade to the train station the next morning seemed to include nearly everyone in town. More than two hundred local rooters joined the players in the sleepers of the special train; then a car was added at Lexington, and two more at Louisville. In that city the *Courier-Journal* proclaimed in a headline that "Kentucky Pins Hopes to Centre College." It is, the article underneath asserted, a battle of "Kentucky, represented by Centre College, against the world!"

Quickly during this week the anticipation spread from the Blue Grass State throughout the South and then to the entire nation. In a rare move, the *New York Times* ran advance stories on the game from Tuesday through Saturday. Howard G. Reynolds of the *Boston Post*, who had so zealously promoted the Colonels the year before, came to Danville again to file column after column and later accompanied the team to Cambridge. Other Boston newspapers filled their sports pages with stories and pictures of the Praying Colonels. A writer for the *Detroit News* summarized all the ballyhoo in his town and elsewhere succinctly: "The football world will turn its eyes to Cambridge this week end." As the special train made its way from Danville to Boston, through Washington and New York, thousands of fans turned out at stations along the way to cheer the clean living young men from Centre College who had given college football a new dimension. The Colonels made no pretense of neutrality in the presidential election less than two weeks away. Banners for the Democratic candidate, James A. Cox, were defiantly plastered over the outside of their Pullman car, and the Kentucky delegation boasted that not a man of them supported the Republican Warren G. Harding.

In Boston a crowd of five hundred alumni and others greeted the team at the station Friday afternoon. So many Centre faculty and students arrived on the same train that the *Boston Herald* sarcastically editorialized that this Kentucky college had solved the problem of football interfering with studies by suspending "academic operations altogether when the gridiron warriors hit the trail." After checking in at a Boston hotel, the Colonels went directly to the Harvard Stadium to practice. For players whose dusty home field had wooden stands seating a few thousand, the sight of this huge stadium, modeled on the ancient stadiums of Greece and Rome, was in itself intimidating. But their awe increased as they waited on the sidelines for Harvard to finish its practice and watched three complete Crimson teams, all seemingly equally heavy, run through their drills. By the end of practice so many fans had come to get a look at the celebrated Praying Colonels that the players had to fight their way through the crowd to reach the locker room. Harvard students themselves seemed caught up in the drama of this game. They entertained the team royally at a Friday evening dinner and dance. Moran rushed the players off to bed at nine, but hours later some seven hundred Kentucky fans, wearing gold and white badges or carrying Centre banners, were still drinking, boasting, and betting as they made the rounds of Boston nightspots.

The demand for tickets for Saturday's game had led to the erection of temporary stands at the unenclosed end of the stadium and the selling of seats on the roof. Some forty-two thousand managed to get in but ten thousand more had to be turned away. Supporters of the Colonels had initially tried to get three to one odds from overconfident Harvard fans. Then, as game time neared, Kentucky pride overcame caution. Some even wagered that Bo McMillin would score more points himself than the entire Harvard team. One Centre student, who had hidden himself on the train to save buying a ticket, bet every cent he had except for enough to buy a sandwich after the game. A telegram to McMillin on Saturday morning from the governor of Kentucky left no doubt as to what was at stake in this contest: "The men in Kentucky are pulling for you, the women are praying for you, the heart of every girl is with you. For God's sake make good! Hit the line hard and low!"

When the Colonels took the field, their pale golden jerseys on top of tattered and torn moleskin pants, already worn out in the first three games, reflected sharply the contrast in resources of the two colleges. As Harvard kicked off to Centre and McMillin ran the ball back fifteen yards, the roar of approval from the stands made it seem that the Kentucky team was playing before a home crowd. By tradition, as many as half of the crowd at Harvard football games bought a ticket for the pleasure of good-naturedly booing the elitist Crimson. Harvard graduate students from other sections of the country were notorious for sitting in the opponent's cheering section. One area of the stands contained hundreds from Boston College who had come to cheer for Centre as a way of avenging Harvard's refusal, snobbish so they thought, to meet the strong team from this neighboring college. Above the roar, the rebel yells of the Kentuckians could be heard answering cheers from the Harvard stands. Despite such an opening ovation, Centre failed to gain and had to punt, after which the Crimson began a sustained drive with its heavier line opening large holes. The overeager Colonels aided their opponent's advance with offside and holding infractions. Within five minutes Harvard plunged over for a touchdown, kicked goal (as the try for point after was then known), and led 7-0.

This easy score brought the Colonels down to earth after the initial excitement — perhaps stage fright — of playing before a crowd larger than any city in Kentucky except Louisville. Their captain began a drive with a twenty-yard run around left end and then opened up the Crimson defense with a pass completed for the same distance. A series of successful end sweeps and small gains through the line brought the ball to the Harvard two-yard line, from which Roberts scored in two plays. Weaver kicked goal to tie the score at 7-7. Harvard had been scored on for the first time of the season. The resulting cheer in the stadium was nearly as pandemonic as the uproar in Danville and the other Kentucky towns where crowds gathered to hear the play-by-play reports.

Harvard selected the option of kicking off, and the quarter ended with the Colonels on their own thirty-two yard line. A holding penalty pushed them back to the seventeen, and two running plays failed to bring a first down. Faking a punt, McMillin threw a pass over forty yards to his fleet halfback, Edwin A. "Lefty" Whitnell, who eluded the few Harvard tacklers not drawn in on the deception, and sprinted the remaining distance to the goal line. This play, sensational by the football standards of that day, brought even the most devoted Harvard rooters to their feet to cheer for the upstart team from Kentucky. In time, the legend of Bo McMillin incorporated the unlikely story that, as this pass sailed through the air before reaching the receiver, he called to his teammates on the sidelines, "Tell the boys to go collect their bets." More certain, Weaver kicked goal, and the incredible news was telegraphed throughout the country that Centre was ahead of Harvard, 14-7.

Ecstatic with their success, the Colonels now went all out to clinch the victory while Harvard, relying on its superior strength, played a waiting game and punted on the second play after receiving the kickoff. In a frantic series of downs, Centre reached its opponent's forty yard line, only to be pushed back fifteen yards for holding with a penalty loudly booed by most of the spectators. A trick running play and a forward pass failed, and a poor punt gave the ball to Harvard on its thirty-seven yard line. The Crimson's superior line began to tell as it repeatedly opened large holes for its backs. Time after time McMillin was left as the only defender between the ball carrier and the goal line. His desperation tackles were as sensational as his running and passing on offense. But Harvard scored without giving up the ball, and the half ended with the game tied, 14-14.

During the halftime intermission, the Colonels surprised everyone by remaining on the field instead of going to the locker room as did Harvard. Draped in bright green blankets, they sat in a circle in the middle of the field while Moran lectured them on the overeagerness that had produced so many penalties. Moran did not mince words; he had to motivate a team already weary and battered, which had played one of the greatest halves of football ever seen in Harvard Stadium. Red Weaver had fought the battle of his football career as he tried to support himself on crippled knees against a defensive center who outweighed him by forty pounds. Both Roberts and McMillin were more badly bruised than they admitted. There was little that Thad McDonnell, the student trainer, could do to ease these aching bodies.

On the kickoff of the second half, Lefty Whitnell was injured and replaced at halfback by Joe Murphy, who at 130 pounds was reputed to be the smallest player who had ever taken the field in Harvard Stadium. McMillin had overheard the Harvard quarterback tell his teammates earlier, "Wait for the breaks, boys; we'll get one in a minute." That break now came after three plays as Murphy's punt went off the side of his foot to give Harvard the ball on Centre's thirty-three yard line, from which the Crimson quickly scored. From then on Centre's frantic efforts to catch up resulted in penalties and intercepted passes that assisted Harvard in scoring another touchdown and a field goal. The stands cheered Centre on to a late fourth quarter drive that was not stopped until reaching Harvard's four-yard line. The contest that ended 31-14 had been, as one writer observed, "a case of David meeting Goliath without the intervention of Providence."

Centre had won everything but the game. It was still the "Magic Team" heralded on the sport pages of the nation for its "great battle." "Why yearn for victory," a Louisville sports writer consoled Kentuckians, "when Centre's triumph over hearts is more lasting and more to be desired?" And Bo McMillin was more of a hero than ever in the eyes of the luminaries of sport journalism who had filled the press box for the game. He had run for 153 yards and passed for 131. On defense he had seemed to be in on every tackle. Grantland Rice was not alone in thinking that this was Bo's greatest game. But it was his character as much as his performance that attracted fans to him. Newspapers across the country featured the scene in the Centre locker room after the game when Arnold Horween, the Harvard captain, came in to offer Bo the game ball because "you are the greatest backfield player I ever saw." His eyes filled with tears as he thanked Horween for such unprecedented sportsmanship but declined because he could not accept a trophy he had not won. Next year, he promised, Centre would be back and win; then he could rightfully take home the game ball. As

the referee and many others who had witnessed the contest acknowledged, this hard-fought game had been a showcase of exemplary
sportsmanship in which the best features of American football had
been put on display for the entire nation.

Danville declared Monday a holiday, and thousands turned out to
hoist the Colonels on shoulders for a parade from the train station
through the town. But the weary and bruised players had little time for
relaxation. Next Saturday, they were scheduled to meet Georgia Tech
in Atlanta. Traveling fifty hours in twelve days, in addition to playing
two games, trying to keep up with classwork, and in some cases working at campus jobs, was too much for even such heroes as Kentucky
considered these "sons of Daniel Boone" to be. Tech had lost only one
game and had a deserved reputation for rough play. With Roberts,
Weaver, and Chinn too injured to start, McMillin slowed from injuries
received last Saturday, and another regular declared ineligible, Centre's prospects seemed unpromising. Nonetheless, the two carloads of
rooters who accompanied the team to Atlanta remained confident and
bet heavily on their favorite. Word of a possible upset had drawn so
many professional gamblers that local authorities placed them under
surveillance.

Before 22,000, the largest crowd that had ever seen a football game
in the South, Georgia Tech manhandled Centre 24-0. Some of the
Tech players had boasted that they were out to get McMillin and knock
off the proud Colonels. A rowdy crowd of Georgians and a band of
five drums increased the volume whenever McMillin called signals.
Fumbles, intercepted passes, and more injuries completely halted the
Colonels' offense. As they fell behind, Weaver returned to his center
position, only to be hurt again. Roberts sought to save the day by putting on the uniform that he had hidden in his luggage after Moran had
forbidden him to bring it. Torn between admiration of this great player's determination to play and anger at his disobedience of an order,
the coach let him punt but not carry the ball. McMillin was kicked in
the head — deliberately, according to his teammates — and dazed, but
no penalty was called. During the next weeks, Kentucky newspapers
denounced Tech's dirty play and "win at any cost" policy and pointed
to the contrasting sportsmanship of the Colonels. Centre College announced that it would never play Georgia Tech again. Once more by

losing, McMillin and his teammates had won the respect of the football world.

The week after they returned from Atlanta, the Centre players joined the hundreds from Danville and nearby towns who twice filled the local movie house to see the complete Harvard game projected on the silver screen. The next Saturday, Indianapolis, its downtown stores decked in Centre's gold and white colors, gave the Colonels a warm welcome for their game with DePauw. This opponent, unscored on this season except by Purdue, promised an upset. But McMillin led his team to a 34-0 victory while dazzling the 10,000 spectators with his running and passing. Crowds of similar size and enthusiasm watched Centre crush Kentucky at Lexington, Virginia Polytechnic Institute at Louisville, and Georgetown at Danville to end the regular season.

Never before had the region seen such enthusiasm for football. Bo McMillin was mobbed by admirers wherever he appeared. Crowds of boys followed him through the streets. The team's halftime sessions in the middle of the field in the last four games had had to be conducted inside a cordon of policemen. Bo became the featured speaker at the banquets given to honor the team. He took the podium even after the coaches and president. His message never altered: with self-sacrifice and rigorous training, his teammates could defeat Harvard next fall. President Ganfield quipped that whereas in the past he had been introduced as the president of Centre College, now he was introduced as the president of Bo McMillin's football team. At the final banquet, given by the Danville Chamber of Commerce, Governor Edwin P. Morrow appointed the Centre quarterback a colonel on his staff, Kentucky's highest honor. From now on he would be *Colonel* Bo McMillin.

Kentuckians expressed disappointment when Walter Camp's All-American selections placed McMillin at quarterback only on the second team. They pointed to his being on the first team chosen by most other football pundits. These All-American backfields usually included George Gipp of Notre Dame, who would die this December and pass into football immortality through Knute Rockne's mythical account of his player's dying words. After all the selections had been made, no doubt remained in the Blue Grass region that Colonel Bo, the adopted son of Kentucky, was the best and most exciting player in the nation.

Centre was in great demand for post-season games, but the faculty asserted itself and limited the team to one game, a much-heralded contest against undefeated Texas Christian University at Fort Worth on New Year's Day. Arriving there before Christmas, the five Colonels from Fort Worth — McMillin, Weaver, Ralph Montgomery, Bill James, and Thad McDonnell — were hailed as returning local heroes. They visited their alma mater, North Side High School, where McMillin was called on to speak to the students. His words delighted his former teachers by urging the boys to pay more attention to studies than to athletics: "Honor in sports is all right, but when you finish school the sports thing becomes only a memory, and unless you've studied hard, the time at school or college" will be "sheer waste." This message may have seemed unconvincing a few days later to these North Side boys as they watched the speaker score four touchdowns in a 63-7 rout of Texas Christian and marveled as Red Weaver kicked goal for the ninety-ninth consecutive time. During their stay in Fort Worth, the Colonels rode in new automobiles supplied by a local dealer. Weaver's mother gave the team a farewell party that provided a fitting valediction for her son's football career. Likely the lightest All-American center in football history, Weaver had finally been forced to admit that his crumpled knees, even supported by the braces he wore, could not withstand another season of battering.

By now McMillin had consciously or unconsciously mastered the art of living the legend that had been created for him. He always said and appeared to do what the public had come to expect of the idealized hero portrayed in the press and by the word-of-mouth stories that made him a nationwide subject of conversation. He was fast becoming a role model held up to young boys by fathers and mothers attempting to steer their sons clear of the shoals of these rapidly changing times. Yet the rigors of his boyhood had deeply embedded another strain in his character, revealed in his urging others to study while neglecting his own classes, in his remaining an inveterate gambler while eschewing other vices, and in his conspicuous frugality, admirable in a college student but laughable in his affluent later years. After proclaiming for months that his greatest ambition was to return to Centre next season to beat Harvard, in January he traveled to Canton, Ohio, to consider an offer to play professional football with the Canton Bulldogs in the newly formed American Professional Football Association, forerunner of the National Football League. The temptation to play for pay with the fabulous Jim Thorpe overwhelmed his loyalty to Centre for weeks. He never revealed the details of the offer, but it was probably no more than the $2,500 offered Thorpe, and it may have been only a game-by-game stipend. Quickly though, the report spread that he had been offered $10,000.

Whatever the monetary inducement, he waited until March to make a final decision. It is quite possible that, at this point if not earlier, the college made him some sort of financial offer.

Meanwhile, the Centre basketball team was in great demand. Football fans crowded into gymnasiums to see — possibly for the last time in a Centre uniform — the famous Colonel Bo at forward. After losing only one game to regional opponents, the team of eight set off in March on an eastern tour that added to Centre's renown and kept McMillin's name on the sports pages. In the single week of 7 March, the boys from Danville defeated the basketball teams of Harvard, Brown, and Johns Hopkins. Bo was lionized at each stop. In a dramatic moment during the game with Harvard, the spectators erupted in cheers when it was announced that he had turned down the professional offer to remain another year at Centre — and play Harvard once more. The tour included a stop in New York City where Bo received admirers at his hotel and was given a banquet and theater party by two hundred grateful Centre alumni. By now his personality attracted as much attention as his athletic exploits. In April he was the main speaker at Syracuse University's annual athletic dinner, where he held the attention of coaches and athletes alike with tales of the Praying Colonels.

The Centre commencement of 1921 mixed sadness and pleasure for McMillin. Students elected him king of the annual Carnival, or as they liked to quip, promoted him from colonel to king. But he had to say goodbye to his teammate of the last seven years, Red Weaver, who had taken a high school coaching position. The week before the festivities his mother, Mattie McMillin, was killed instantly on 30 May in Fort Worth when hit by an automobile. The funeral brought the family together again and provided a reminder of how hard their mother had fought to set her children on the right path.

A grieving Bo went off to his summer job with the Chautauqua. He was now the advance agent who arranged for and publicized the coming attraction of this cultural institution. His athletic fame made him an unusually welcome pitchman. A reporter who noted his talk in a chapel service of the Bowling Green, Kentucky, "Business University" wrote that Bo, despite being a "household word," is a "simple, modest, unassuming gentleman....[who] possesses characteristics other than gridiron prowess that will win for him even higher honors than he has achieved heretofore....His ability to translate the enthusiasm, the determination and the clean sportsmanship of this game into terms of business life held the close attention of every student who heard him this morning....His talk was permeated with the vigor and 'pep' which he puts into football contests."

The legend of Bo McMillin was amplified when *First Down Kentucky* came off the press late in August. Ralph Delahaye Paine (Yale '94), after a career as a war correspondent and muckraking journalist, had turned to writing adventure and sports stories for boys. His popular books, particularly those based on naval history, had made him one of the best known "pulp" writers in the United States. Intrigued with the rise to fame of the Praying Colonels, he had visited Danville during the 1920 football season to gather information for a book. The result was a biographical novel closely following the life of the Centre quarterback through the first game against Harvard. Paine added some touches typical of sports fiction of his day: a pure romance for Bo with a Fort Worth girl of one of the best families; a "big hearted and husky" father who, although uneducated and only a "first class mechanic," had risen to hardware manufacturer; and a winning battle to outwit professional gamblers. Above all, Paine pictured Bo McMillin as a young man with whom "a point of honor is never debatable."

Knowing that McMillin had enlisted in the navy, Paine turned him into a hero of World War I. In *First Down Kentucky*, Bowman McMurray (Bo McMillin) suffered a serious foot wound and spent a night in the ocean after his destroyer was torpedoed by a German submarine. His football days seemingly over, he gave thought to a career in the navy and recovered sufficiently to be sent back to sea. As his new destroyer went into combat, he took over the wheel from a dazed helmsman and held the ship on its battle course through a smoke screen even as it cut in two another vessel that had strayed off its course. Then Colonel Shelby, "the first citizen of Sommersworth [Somerset], Kentucky," personally persuaded the secretary of the navy to discharge Bowman so he could have his ankle repaired by "an eminent surgeon in Washington." Following a successful operation, the fictional hero returned to Centre College, a greater man than ever.

Among all this pulp, Paine revealed clearly the meaning of Centre's game with Harvard in a conversation between Bowman McMurray (McMillin) and Andy Swope (Moran):

> "I reckon Harvard is an unfortunate mental attitude," observed Bowman. "Does it wear off in after life, like being a second lieutenant?"
>
> "If they get out into the United States it does, Bo, but not if they stay in Boston. Of course, they know who Princeton is. The wilderness begins west of New Jersey, but as for queer little colleges like us, 'way out in No Man's Land,' they'd be liable to ask if we graduated barbers, stenographers, or banjo players."

In 1921, nearly a century after the election of Andrew Jackson to the presidency had supposedly ushered in the age of the common man, Harvard College still symbolized aristocracy "west of New Jersey." As Paine recognized, Centre College had for the moment become the surrogate alma mater of those Americans who retained shades of Jackson's disdain for — and perhaps fear of — eastern sophistication and elitism. Hundreds of thousands of boys read *First Down Kentucky*, most as it was serialized in five parts by the semi-monthly *Popular Magazine*. They too could dream of becoming giant killers like Bo McMillin, and their parents encouraged such dreams.

CHAPTER FOUR

Centre 6 — Harvard 0

(1921)

Centre College has a tradition, a magnificent burst of greatness after World War I that culminated in the football game that captivated the country. The date was October 29, 1921. The score was Centre 6, Harvard 0. What made the score so stunning was that Harvard was national champion, unbeaten in five seasons, and Centre was...a tiny liberal arts college in central Kentucky.

New York Times (1971: on the
fiftieth anniversary of this game)

Once Bo McMillin had resisted the temptation to turn professional, his all-consuming goal became to avenge last year's loss at Cambridge. Four years of gridiron success and national fame could not entirely heal the hurt his ego had suffered from the 31-14 defeat before the eyes of the nation. He had said that he would come back next year and take home the game ball, and now he lived for nothing else. The entire college community and much of Kentucky also focused all attention on this one contest.

Playing that game without McMillin was inconceivable, and it appears that the college administration stretched the eligibility rules to let him play. A year before, the players had been warned that the Southern Intercollegiate Athletic Association had ruled that they must pass three courses in the winter semester to be eligible for football the next fall. As the season opened, Chief Myers was quoted as stating that "we stand to lose a number of last year's squad through failure to keep up in their classes." Most conspicuous among the ineligible was "Lefty" Whitnell, who had scored a touchdown against Harvard. Yet there was no explanation of why McMillin, who had taken only three courses in the last semester and failed one, was permitted to play. At the beginning of his fifth year at Centre, he was still 35 credits short of the 120 required for graduation. Perhaps the quarterback quieted faculty objections when he registered in September for five solid courses. The professors, for the most part, seemed as caught up in football mania as the president and alumni and may have easily been persuaded, perhaps by the president, to relax their standards for the glory of Old Centre. Whatever the rationale, there was not the slightest whisper in Danville that the hero of *First Down Kentucky* was in academic difficulty.

McMillin had refused to be captain for a third year, and the honor went to "Army" Armstrong. The evident weakness of the Centre line against Harvard in 1920 led Coach Moran to employ a line coach, Claude E. "Tiny" Thornhill, who had starred at the University of Pittsburgh and then played professional football. Thornhill had worked with the team briefly before the 1920 Harvard game, so he was able to step in quickly and make significant changes, among them moving the powerful Red Roberts from fullback to the line; and he discovered several capable linemen in the more than one hundred freshmen who had flocked from twenty-one states to the now famous little college in the Bluegrass. When Moran reached the campus at the end of the baseball season, he found three full teams at practice with a notable improvement in their line play, and he no longer had to limit practice scrimmages for fear of injuries to his few regulars. In his tenth year in football, Bo McMillin would play for the first time behind a line that, though averaging a little lighter than last season's, could hold its own with his team's best opponents.

Despite their improvement, the Colonels had to struggle to win against Clemson and Virginia Polytechnic Institute before easier contests with Xavier and Transylvania. In early season practice, McMillin had suffered a blow to the nose, and he reinjured it in the Clemson and VPI games, despite wearing a nose guard. Unable to sleep because of difficulty in breathing, he spent several days in the hospital but got out of bed in time to travel to Cincinnati to play Xavier, much to the delight of the fans in that city, where a sports writer had promoted the game by writing that McMillin is to football what "Jack Dempsey is to boxing,...[and] Babe Ruth to baseball." He eventually recovered from this injury, but the indentation in the bridge of his nose left him looking like the boxer he had intended to be in boyhood.

With each of Centre's victories against other opponents, the excitement over its date in Cambridge on 29 October continued to build in Kentucky, where, as the *Louisville Courier-Journal* noted, "the chief question is — Will Centre be able to beat Harvard this year?" The Boston newspapers hyped the game as they had done in 1920. Although the Crimson had not been beaten since a 6-3 loss to Yale in 1916, many of its veterans had been graduated, and this season crippling injuries had further weakened the squad. Against Penn State the week before, Harvard had staved off defeat only by a last-minute tie. Still Harvard was Harvard, and even Grantland Rice predicted that Centre would lose by fourteen points. In Cambridge, the Crimson coaches took Centre lightly and prepared instead for the match with Princeton two weeks away. They announced that some of the first team who had been injured would not play against the Kentuckians in order to make sure they were ready for the Ivy League foe. Bo McMillin was disappointed. In a pep talk to his team at the last practice before leaving for Boston, he expressed his fervent hope that all the Crimsons would be recovered from their injuries, for he wanted to beat Harvard at its best.

Sensitive to criticism of its academic standards, the Centre faculty refused to dismiss classes so that professors and students could accompany the team, although the college's five-man band was permitted to go. Nonetheless, the sendoff in 1921 was even more tumultuous than 1920. As they rode East the Colonels could admire over and over their pictures on a full page of last Sunday's rotogravure section of the *Louisville Courier-Journal,* where Colonel Bo was hailed as "Danville's Alexander the Great" leading "an expedition to Cambridge." And they could talk with Howard G. Reynolds as he again accompanied the team to Boston to write stories on the Colonels for the *Boston Post.* But at the stops along the way, the crowds were smaller and the reporters fewer than last year. Outside of Boston and Kentucky, this was just another good game on the coming Saturday's schedule. With Weaver and Whitnell gone, some reporters had concluded that this year's Centre squad was "far inferior" to the team that had tested Harvard in 1920.

When they arrived in Boston Thursday afternoon, the Colonels were met by a crowd that included Albert B. Chandler, known to everyone as "Happy" because he could usually be heard singing when otherwise unoccupied. A student in the Harvard Law School, Chandler had played football against Centre while an undergraduate at Transylvania College. But for him now, like all Kentuckians and many ordinary people, Centre College became his adopted alma mater. He had scouted Harvard's games this season and diagrammed that team's plays for Moran.

Practices at Fenway Park Thursday afternoon and in the Stadium Friday morning left ample time for the Kentuckians to be even more lavishly entertained than the year before. The many who met the famous Bo, now three months shy of his twenty-seventh birthday, seem not to have noticed that he was a man playing with boys. He exuded confidence; a few thought it was arrogance. On one occasion he charged toward a newspaper photographer to demand another picture because he did not like the first pose he had struck. His incessant drawling so intermingled football wisdom with homespun moralisms and humor that anyone who heard him understood what one commentator meant when he wrote of football being Centre College's religion. The Saturday morning *Boston Globe* best expressed his heroic stature by publishing a photograph of a smiling, assured Bo under the caption, "Here He is, Watch Him Go, in the Stadium this Afternoon."

After the Colonels had dressed for the game in their Boston hotel and President Ganfield had prayed, Moran asked Chandler to sing. His rich voice filled the room with the words of "Down the Trail to Home Sweet Home," a song then dear to the hearts of southerners. Before he had finished, Bo McMillin and all his teammates were in tears. With eyes still wet, they climbed into a bus for the ride across the Charles River to the stadium.

The demeanor that the team presented to the 45,000 who crowded into the stadium was not, however, entirely serious. With them had come their combination mascot, water carrier, and masseur, Roscoe Arbuckle Conklin Bloomfield, an older black man reputed to be the champion cakewalker of Kentucky. His skin a deep shade of amber, he was dressed in light trousers, a dark coat over a bright yellow vest, and a top hat. To many Bostonians he seemed the personification of the then familiar advertisement for Kentucky tobacco as he promenaded on the Stadium turf during the pre-game warmups. Throughout the game he nimbly cakewalked on and off the field between plays, and he entertained at halftime. As one observer noted, "spectacled professors and feminine blue-stockings cheered in an altogether unpuritanical fashion as Roscoe cakewalked and pigeon-winged across the gridiron." Nicknamed "Hope to Tell the Truth," he was a great favorite of the players, who had insisted that the College pay his way to Cambridge.

Of all the legends to which this game gave rise, none more endeared itself to later writers than the words attributed to Coach Moran in the huddle before play began: "I know you guys have been royally entertained by these Harvard chaps, but just remember one thing....Everyone of those bums votes the straight Republican ticket." Apocryphal or not, this story pointed to the social significance of richly endowed, aristocratic Harvard College doing gridiron battle with a school whose 250 boys proudly considered themselves the sons of Daniel Boone.

The sixteen "Praying Colonels" who would play in this game of destiny averaged 175 pounds, light even by the football standards of that day, but they were fast and drilled to perfection. Anchoring the backfield with Bo was Norris "Army" Armstrong, whose strong halfback play was matched by his intelligence and good nature. Speedy Terry Snowday (Snoddy) might line up at either end or halfback. Tom Bartlett and John Tanner shared the fullback position, and Herb Covington could fill in at either quarterback or halfback. Ray Class dropkicked and punted. All-American James "Red" Roberts, six feet tall and 210 pounds, moved to end or tackle depending on the play called. Unlike the 1920 game at Cambridge, this year Coach Moran had the luxury of substituting linemen. Although Roberts, Ben Cregor, George Jones, Ed Kubale, and Bill James played nearly every minute, William Shadoan, Dick Gibson, Frank Rubarth, and Minos Gordy saw considerable action.

In 1920, "Uncle Charlie" Moran had hoped that an all-out Centre attack could outscore Harvard. Now he reversed the strategy and ordered his quarterback to call a defensive game to avoid destructive penalties and interceptions while awaiting a break. Harvard had prepared for the open-field running and passing attack Centre had displayed the year before. Instead, they got line smashing, straight football. During the entire afternoon Harvard stuck to its game plan, which included only six standard plays; anything more deceptive was for saved for Princeton and Yale. And the Crimson coach held back several key players for fear that their injuries would be aggravated. Despite the size and noise of the crowd, the plans of the two coaches might have produced a lackluster game between Harvard and most of the teams on its schedule. But a contest between colleges of such disproportionate sizes and resources could never be dull when played before such a crowd, many of whom were eager to see Harvard humbled.

In a scoreless first half, Harvard missed two drop kicks for field goals, and Centre one. Harvard once reached the Colonel's thirteen yard line but was stopped there. Centre then fumbled the ball away on its twenty, but once again prevented a score. The Crimson received the kickoff to begin the second half but failed to advance and had to punt. After a short runback, the Centre receiver was dropped on the Harvard forty-six yard line by overeager tacklers who received a fifteen yard penalty for piling on, thus advancing the ball to the thirty-one. Bo had never forgotten last year's Harvard quarterback urging his team to wait for the breaks to win. Back in the huddle he gave his team the same message: "Boys, this is the break we have been waiting for. Everybody block a little better than you know how on this play, and I'll take her all the way home!"

On the next play, McMillin took the snap from center and darted through the right side of his line, where Red Roberts had opened a wide hole by piling up three would-be tacklers. Once through the line, he reversed his direction and headed for the left corner of the field. No defender had yet touched him as he watched "Baldy" Ben Cregor level the safety man. Ten yards from the goal, along the sideline, two tacklers threw themselves at McMillin to knock him out of bounds. But he stopped so suddenly that they only brushed against his body and went out themselves. His stop and restart enabled several Harvard players to catch him at the goal line. But it was too late. Bo McMillin had scored in a thirty-one yard run that brought all but the most die-hard Harvard fans in the stands screaming to their feet.

Bartlett failed to kick goal, leaving Harvard still confident that it could win with a touchdown and extra point. But an enheartened Centre defense twice forced Crimson punts. Then, while the defenders concentrated on McMillin, the Centre backs Tom Bartlett and Herb Covington made substantial gains, followed by a triple pass that put the ball on the Crimson's eleven yard line as the third quarter ended. Harvard held there after the worried coach inserted some of the men he had not wanted to play. Following an exchange of punts, the Kentucky team was pushed back to its thirty-three in the last few minutes of the game. A pass from a kicking formation seemed certain to score until Roberts and McMillin caught the receiver at the three. With only three yards to go in four plays, the Crimson would likely put over the tying touchdown and kick goal for the win. Centre was saved, however, by an offside penalty called on this play by the head linesman. When he realized that the play had been nullified, McMillin — so the *Boston Globe* reported —"ran across to the flag that marked the spot where the penalty was to be imposed and, dropping to his knees on the sod, with bowed head and hands uplifted together, he rested there a few seconds in the attitude of prayer." This impetuous but sincere act put on display before 45,000 fans the Bo McMillin known in private to his close friends.

The last Harvard hope ended when Bartlett intercepted a pass, a turnover made possible because McMillin had noticed throughout the game that the Crimson ends telegraphed pass plays by glancing at the opposing halfbacks. Centre now kept the ball and was threatening to score again when time ran out. Unaware that the game was over, McMillin charged the referee demanding a penalty on the last play. Since Armstrong had left with an injury, the quarterback was acting captain. The official, the three-hundred-pound Robert W. "Tiny" Maxwell, picked up the ball and said, "Here, take this ball, that's all you'll get." The man who had wanted nothing more in his life than to beat Harvard stood dazed for a few seconds. Then the realization struck home. He grabbed the ball, tossed it to "Happy" Chandler for safekeeping, and began to run in circles, embracing every player and southerner who broke through the police lines and ran on the field. He was smothered by the kisses of his teammates. Hundreds rushed from the stands to insist on carrying him off the field on their shoulders. In the crush, Roscoe Bloomfield was so enthusiastically hoisted on the shoulders of Centre supporters that they broke one of his ribs. He did not mind. For him, and for all the Colonels, this was the supreme moment of their young lives. "I am the happiest man in the world," proclaimed Bo McMillin.

It mattered not that a green Crimson team had played the game seemingly indifferent to the outcome and holding back a few regulars even when behind in the score. Harvard had been beaten in regular play for the first time since 1916, and a tiny southern college had done it! Centre had fired a shot heard 'round the football world. As the *Detroit News* rhapsodized the next day, "Colonel 'Bo' McMillin and his mates have come up from the south and accomplished what everyone had refused to believe was possible." A half century later the *New York Times* commemorated the anniversary of "Football's Upset of the Century" by reprinting a photograph and part of the original article describing Centre's victory, including the star quarterback's declaration that he was "the happiest man in the world." Sportswriter Tim Cohane put it more succinctly in 1973: Centre's defeat of Harvard in 1921 was "an upset that rocked the nation as no other ever had." A Centre alumnus serving with the American Relief Administration in Austria went much further. He wrote, "Vienna received the most important news which has emanated from America in the past seven years, to wit: that Centre College beat Harvard University....It has been flashed to every American Embassy, Legation, and Consulate throughout the world." The significance of the contest at Harvard Stadium on 29 October 1921 was perhaps best caught in one stanza of a verse by an unknown poet who wrote that it was the story of "How just a wee small college/ Had the everlasting gall/ To try to show fair Harvard/How to play football."

Nor did it matter that this victory had resulted from the exceptional play of a half dozen of McMillin's teammates who deserved equal credit with him. His touchdown run immortalized "the pride of Texas, Kentucky and the entire Southland" as the David in cleats who had brought down John Harvard, the Goliath of football. Back at the hotel that evening he was showered with kisses by the beauties of the Ziegfield Follies while he tried to sign autographs for a horde of admirers and read the telegrams of congratulations from dozens of important and ordinary people. As the "Sportsman" in the *Boston Globe* explained, "George Bernard Shaw may never have heard of Bo McMillin, but his name is on the lips of all the kids of this broad land and he is an outstanding figure with all red-blooded men and women." A month later the congregation of the First Christian Church of Kansas City, Missouri, heard its minister declare in a sermon that Bo McMillin, "who made the famous run against Harvard, is as clean as a hound's tooth. He is the greatest football player in the world." The preacher climaxed his homily with a strong admonition: "If you wish to succeed in life, you must," like Bo and the Praying Colonels, "make God your coach."

Danville and all of Kentucky were ecstatic. Monday was declared a holiday. Before the train bringing the Colonels home arrived at 11:30 that morning — late because of unscheduled stops along the way to let people cheer the conquerors of Harvard — the newly discovered chemical formula, C^6H^0, had already been painted on many Danville buildings, automobiles, and even on a cow. Governor Edwin P. Morrow headed a welcoming crowd of thousands, many from surrounding towns. With Roscoe leading the parade from the station, the players rode on the town's fire engine, on top of which perched Colonel McMillin with the precious game ball tucked under his arm. Speaking from the steps of the court house, the governor drew great applause by declaring that he would willingly change places with McMillin, Roberts, or any of the Colonels, a declaration that the press quickly shortened to "I would rather be Bo McMillin than governor of Kentucky." Long after the official celebration had ended, the parties went on into the night.

There was still a season to finish. In the last regularly scheduled games, four major teams failed to score on the Colonels. All but one played away from Danville, these contests provided more showcases for the talents of McMillin, although there was increasing recognition that the team's success was due nearly as much to Red Roberts. Centre seemed the leading contender for the mythical national championship, and all of Kentucky was proud of the Praying Colonels who "fall on their knees and then on their foes." The most powerful man in the region, Judge Robert Worth Bingham, publisher of the *Louisville Courier-Journal* and its sister newspaper, the *Louisville Times*, gave a dinner dance for the team that became one of the highlights of the social season. A full-length photograph of Colonel Bo was displayed in the window of a sporting goods store in Louisville, and Centre alumni of that city commissioned a portrait of him to be given to the college. Not to be outdone, Danville's social matrons feted their "Wonder Team" with a dinner and composed poetry to their heroes.

Through all the festivities, McMillin expressed tearful thanks for the honors given him, and reporters hung on his words. Would he take it easy in a charity all-star game in in Columbus, Ohio, on Saturday after playing Tulane in New Orleans on Thanksgiving the Thursday before? " 'What!' exclaimed McMillin. 'Do you suppose I made that trip here with any expectation of not winning? I have never started a game in my life in which I didn't expect to win and I certainly expect to win this.' " His team did, 16-0, in a game featured by his eighty-six yard run for a touchdown and another score by Eddie Casey, the famous Harvard halfback. Continuing to cultivate his own legend, McMillin let slip that he had turned down an offer of $1,000 to play a professional game on this Saturday in order to be in Columbus.

At a farewell alumni banquet in Louisville, he burst into tears while declaring, "I would be supremely happy if I could only play with Centre all my life." And he added in words directed to the toastmaster, a former Centre valedictorian, that he "would have gladly given up all the honors that have been accorded him if he knew he would complete his course at the head of his class."

Insisting that McMillin had been better against Harvard in 1920 than 1921, Walter Camp named the Centre quarterback only to his second All-American team while he placed Red Roberts at end on the first team. A number of the other All-American teams placed the two in the same relationship, a belated recognition that Centre's success this season owed much to the powerful blocking of the Colonel who played end, tackle, or fullback as the situation demanded. Yet Kentucky and Boston newspapers insisted in their All-American selections that quarterback Bo was the best in the country.

After an incredible maze of negotiations, rumors, and innuendos concerning the eligibility of players on teams considered for post-season games, Centre eventually turned down the opportunity to play in the Rose Bowl in favor of the more financially rewarding East-West game against the University of Arizona at San Diego on 26 December. In addition, the Colonels contracted to play Texas A & M at Dallas on 2 January in the Dixie Classic, forerunner of the Cotton Bowl.

Twenty-two lettermen left Danville on 16 December for what the college yearbook called "their triumphant march across the country," during which "at every station they were met by crowds of people" as "Kentuckians everywhere did their best to entertain them in true Kentucky style." Kentucky's leading newspapers followed the team day by day. During a stop in Hollywood, while Captain Armstrong and Uncle Charlie Moran looked on, Bo McMillin was photographed as he playfully tackled the movie queen, Gloria Swanson, who had obligingly tucked a football under the arm of her stylish, jazz era dress. The Praying Colonels attracted so much interest in Hollywood that several movie stars followed them to San Diego for the game and socialized with the players on the train and in the hotel. And San Diego welcomed the Colonels as conquering heroes. The town's morning newspaper turned out a Centre College edition with the entire front page devoted to the team.

In the East-West game, played despite torrential rains and heavy fog, Centre defeated the Southwestern Conference champion 38-0. But the weather did not dampen the spirits of the victors, who, with Kentuckians living nearby and fans from Hollywood, celebrated in the Hotel Del Coronado until 2:00 a.m. The downpour washed out some railroad tracks near San Diego and threatened the team's arrival in Los Angeles before the scheduled departure for Dallas. McMillin could not take that chance. Before he knew of the game on January second, his wedding had been set for that day, and he wanted to be in Fort Worth in time to attend the pre-wedding events already planned. An obliging naval officer eased the bridegroom's mind by giving him a ride on a destroyer going to Los Angeles. There, however, the team caught up in time to make the train.

Monday, 2 January 1922, symbolized an important transition in the life of Bo McMillin. That morning he was married, and that afternoon he played his last college football game. He in effect changed one family for another. Chief Myers had been his surrogate father for ten years. Now he took a wife and would soon begin a family of his own. His bride, Marie Miers, a few months older than Bo, had been another pillar of his life since he began courting her during their high school days. Born in Indiana, she had moved to Fort Worth with her parents and attended school there. Like Bo, she had lost her father and now lived with a widowed mother. And like Bo also, wherever she went, her warm personality drew friends and admirers to her. They had enjoyed an idealized romance that fitted perfectly with the public image of the football hero. The symbolism of this day, however, was marred by the fate of athletes who overreach themselves.

They were married at nine in the morning before a crowd of hundreds in All Saints, the family church in Fort Worth. Following a nuptial high mass and a wedding breakfast at the McMillin home, the couple and the team motored the thirty miles to Dallas for the game. In the locker room a tearful bridegroom, overcome by the emotion of playing his last game for the Gold and White, offered a prayer in which he gave thanks to God "for the place Old Centre has attained in the athletic world." Then, with Marie on his arm, he led the team onto the field, where she sat on the bench with the Centre team. The bride's smiles turned to tears at game's end. After two weeks in Pullman cars, lavish entertainment, changes in climate, and the excitement of the wedding that morning, the exhausted, stale, but still overconfident Praying Colonels needed more than prayer to beat the Texas Aggies, whose coach, Dana X. Bible, had carefully prepared his team to spring an upset. To make matters worse, Roberts wrenched his knee at the start and had to play crippled. The contest ended 22-14 against Centre. The new husband had given the worst performance of his career and would long regret that this was the last college game Marie would see him play. Gone was Centre's claim to the national championship. The team from Danville had been a four to one favorite; thus rumors spread that some of the boys had sold out to gamblers. And not a few back in Kentucky wondered whether the Praying Colonels had become the "Drinking Colonels."

The bitter taste of this final game soon left the mouths of the Praying Colonels of 1921, who would for the remainder of their lives think of themselves and be known to others as the team that had beaten Harvard. Most would go on to successful but quiet careers in business, education, and the professions. Only a few "missed the signal" in the game of life, as Captain Norris Armstrong recapitulated in old age. No such obscurity lay ahead for Bo McMillin. His life would be spent in seeking new giants to slay.

CHAPTER FIVE

My Pore Lil' Boys

(1921-1934)

*Bo was loved by all the players; he was more like a father
than a coach to the players. I have always said he was
worth his salary to the college, even if he didn't coach, just
to have his influence on the boys.... You would be surprised how those lessons stayed with most of the boys all
the rest of their lives.*

Calvin Hubbard

Until his triumph in Harvard Stadium, the life of Bo McMillin had followed closely the classic pattern of the heroes of sports novels for boys. Springing from an unpromising origin, he had been set on
the right road by a dedicated coach with high ideals. Then through
hard work, devotion to his college, loyalty to teammates, and strict
morals, he had risen to the pinnacle of success as the most celebrated
football player in a nation increasingly fanatical about contests on college gridirons. The novels, however, ended with the apotheosis of the
storybook hero, thus leaving the reader with the illusion that an
equally glorious adulthood would naturally follow. In real life though,
as countless biographies testify, heroes of sport often faded into obscurity and failed to capitalize on their evanescent fame.

But McMillin differed in an important respect from most sport heroes. His years at Centre had fused in his being the legendary and the
real man. He perceived himself as the press, adoring Centre students,
and alumni described him: a man of phenomenal athletic ability, natural leadership, high moral character, genuine piety, and unselfish devotion to family, friends, and associates. Thus, whatever lay ahead for
him, he could play no new role; he would always be the giant killer

whose character was as important in his heroic stature as his gridiron prowess. As much as a few later critics saw his contributions to his own legend as self-serving, those who knew him best seem never to have doubted the sincerity of this role. It was the character of the man that made his post-college career a continuation, though usually to a smaller audience, of those fabulous five years in the Kentucky Bluegrass.

The philosophy of life first taught McMillin by Chief Myers and reinforced at Centre promised that success would come to the man of hard work and good character. Thus it is not surprising that while he played out the remainder of the 1921 football season, this nationally renowned athlete, nearing the end of his twenty-sixth year, had been thinking of compensating for his late start in college by turning his fame into cash. To marry the Fort Worth girl he had courted for eight years, much of the time at a distance of 800 miles, demanded a steady income. As Centre finished its season, the question of "Where will Bo go next?" made the headlines of Kentucky newspapers and occupied much of his thought.

The "crying quarterback" had neglected his studies while playing and interviewing for coaching positions. Several southern colleges had jumped at the opportunity to hire the famous Bo and, like Centre, rise to gridiron glory. His presence, it was believed, would attract to any campus, however small and remote, recruits for a winning team. In mid-December an offer too good to refuse had come from tiny Centenary College in Shreveport, Louisiana, and he signed a contract to coach for three years at a salary of $8,000 — the press reported $10,000. It seemed like a fortune to one who still considered himself a poor boy from Texas.

With a wife to support, McMillin turned professional the week after his last college game by playing in exhibition games in Fort Worth and San Antonio. By the time he returned to Danville, his first semester courses were hopelessly lost, and he failed all five. But he had promised to coach basketball and track for Centre in the winter and spring of 1922, so he took an apartment and registered for four courses (three in economics). He soon found himself as absorbed in coaching as in playing and with little time for his studies. At the end of the track season he was no closer to his degree than a year ago. He departed Centre promising to come back and finish some day, a promise that in the

1922 commencement season drew only knowing smiles from his classmates and the faculty.

Proud of his accomplishments at Centre College, President Ganfield left Kentucky shortly before Bo McMillin to become president of Carroll College in Wisconsin, where, he told a reporter, he planned to develop a football team that would beat the University of Wisconsin. Ganfield's departure came amid a growing wave of criticism around the nation of the overemphasis on football by American colleges such as Centre, as the new coach of Centenary would soon discover.

Colonel and Mrs. McMillin received a royal welcome in Shreveport, where he was expected to produce at Centenary "another wonder squad, a mighty eleven out of a mite of a team." The oldest liberal arts college west of the Mississippi, the school's roots in Louisiana went back to 1825. It had soon become affiliated with the Methodist Church and in 1908 had been moved to Shreveport in the northwestern corner of the state. World War I had crippled the college, which in 1920-1921 had only seven members of the faculty, three buildings, and forty-three students. A group of leading Shreveport citizens had determined to save Centenary and persuaded a popular local minister, George S. Sexton, to assume the presidency. He had set to work to attract students and increase the endowment: in other words, to make Centenary another Centre, an example he knew well. Although the college had a capable young coach, Homer Norton, the new president wanted instant gridiron success. He had delegated Laura Bishop, Bo's teacher from Fort Worth, now on the Centenary faculty, to approach her former pupil with whom she had corresponded during his college years. Her telegram to him had brought a quick response: "Can you beat the offer of $7,000 of Dallas University?" He had asked also for a three-year contract. Affirmative answers from Centenary had sealed the deal. His salary of $8,000 would be paid by the citizens group, not the college. Thus the December 1921 edition of the student newspaper could proclaim, "The brightest satellite in the athletic world has been presented to Centenary College as a Christmas present."

His was not the highest coaching salary in the nation, but it was far better than most and shockingly high for a beginning coach at a Southern institution of Centenary's size and means. Without a degree or coaching experience, he would be paid more than the president and three times what most faculty received. In addition, he expected to augment his salary by playing an occasional professional game. Already, it was reported, he commanded at least $500 a game and had received $2,000 for one. His sudden prosperity overwhelmed his inbred frugality for perhaps the only time in his life. He bought the largest automobile he could find, a green Cadillac, a luxury his conscience did not let him enjoy for long.

Once he knew that his best offer had come from a tiny institution, McMillin could easily harmonize his acceptance with his public image. In a series of nationally syndicated newspaper articles, he wrote that in order to coach in college he had turned down "flattering offers" from professional teams and that his Centre experience had better prepared him for the environment of a small school. He wanted a squad of a size where he could "know all of my boys personally" rather than merely directing "a bunch of assistants" in a large school where "a football team is more like some mechanical device." In President Sexton, he wrote, he had found a man whose educational ideals were similar to his own. "We hope to put Centenary College on the football map if it can be done by good clean athletics. However, the main thought is the development of the young manhood of the college and to turn out men who will be a credit to both the college and the nation." Myers had taught his protégé well.

From his first days as a coach at Centenary, McMillin combined the best he had learned from Chief Myers and Uncle Charlie Moran. On the field, he drove his players beyond the limits of their ability. He put on the pads for scrimmages in which he taught by example. He tackled and blocked harder than anyone else and offered prizes to tacklers who could bring him down when he ran with the ball. Once over their initial awe of him, they came to admire his coaching skills, particularly in developing new, unorthodox plays and designing special defenses for the next opponent. Off the field, he became their father, sharing their lives through joys and sorrows, while all the time demanding strict adherence to his code of conduct. With his arrival, the college's athletic teams had been renamed the "Gentlemen," and he expected their conduct to match the name. Yet, out of sight of the press and college officials, he was always "Bo" to his boys. He lived only for football. His intensity made it nearly impossible to sleep the night before a game or to eat on game days. In any social gathering he could be counted on to draw a crowd into a corner to discuss teams and illustrate plays with dishes, bric-a-brac, or whatever he could find. The Shreveport backers of Centenary football knew almost from the beginning that they would get their money's worth.

The well-publicized hiring of a famous coach helped to triple the college's enrollment for the fall of 1922. Aspiring football players came from several states. Among them was a man destined for athletic greatness. While with his Centre team at a track meet in Missouri last spring, McMillin had been approached by a large twenty-year-old who insisted that he was going to play football wherever the hero of the Praying Colonels coached. True to his word, Robert Calvin Hubbard—well over six feet, 240 pounds and still growing, and with a sprinter's speed — enrolled at Centenary in the fall and brought another player with him. A half century later he would still rank as one of the greatest linemen of all time. Now he was just a country boy so eager to get into college football that he gave up cigarettes and profanity to play for the coach he idolized.

The seriousness of Centenary's football plans became further evident when McMillin and assistant coach Norton took their players in August to a summer camp in the Ozarks and then brought them home to Shreveport to a loud welcome from local citizens. Although the coaches had to depend mostly on freshmen, their squad, with a line averaging 200 pounds, was of good size for that day. Hubbard, playing tackle on offense and linebacker on defense, was alone enough to dominate most of the teams on Centenary's previously arranged schedule. In the 1922 season, the Gentlemen scored 295 points to their opponent's 41, and lost only to the University of Tennessee. But Colonel McMillin was hunting for bigger game.

Two major teams, Texas Christian University and Boston College, were added to the 1923 schedule. McMillin brought his close friend and former high school teammate, Rosco Minton, to Centenary as another assistant coach. From a student body now swelled to 290, there were 50 candidates from whom to select a squad. After four easy victories, the Gentlemen went to Fort Worth, where they defeated Matty Bell's TCU Horn Frogs 23-0 in a contest featured by the newspapers as a battle between the two mentors. This seemed a particularly gratifying victory to McMillin, who may have still harbored some resentment over the scholarly Bell's refusal to return to Centre for the second battle against Harvard. In any case, the game displayed before their home town fans two of Chief Myers' former North Siders who were on their way to becoming famed coaches as well as star players.

Getting a game with Boston College for 10 November 1923 in that city where he had been so celebrated was the master stroke of McMillin's campaign to bring Centenary to national attention. Howard G. Reynolds of the *Boston Post* took the lead in promoting this game, as he had done for the Harvard-Centre clashes. But Boston needed no introduction to Colonel Bo. He was welcomed as a returning hero and presented the key to the city by the mayor. Under Coach Frank Cavanagh, the Boston College Eagles had emerged as an eastern football power. He was a determined, some said ruthless, coach who believed that football "should be played to the uttermost limits of respectability."

The hero of little Centre's conquest of Harvard came to Boston playing the David versus Goliath theme for all it was worth. His team, McMillin drawled endlessly, was made up of "pore lil' country boys," gathered from the shadows of Centenary's Old Main and much too small to play teams like the Eagles. Cavanagh scoffed. That shadow, he reminded Bo, would have to reach to Missouri to cover Cal Hubbard and to a half dozen other states from which Centenary drew players. And Grantland Rice delighted in reporting the weights of the "lil'" giants on the Centenary front line. But good-natured teasing never diminished Colonel Bo's emphasis on the major theme of his college coaching: 'pore lil' country boys" who lived clean, trained hard, and stuck together could win in both football and life. By no coincidence, Grantland Rice's poem "Bill Jones," now entitled "The Game of Life," appeared in the Centenary senior yearbook in the section on football for that season.

Before 23,000 in Braves Field, Centenary lost to Boston College Eagles, 14-0. An injury to Cal Hubbard early in the game and poor kicking were mainly responsible for the loss. Nonetheless, the Gentlemen came home to a tumultuous welcome from citizens of Shreveport, now thoroughly awakened to the excitement of intersectional football. Coach McMillin assumed the blame for his team's poor play and promised a win next year, because "a Gentleman will not take a licking." He kept his promise when Centenary went back to Boston to beat the Eagles 10-9 on 15 November 1924.

By the end of his third season at Centenary, McMillin's teams had won twenty-five games and lost only three. The Gentlemen were now one of the "Big Four" in southern football. Both the college and the town of Shreveport had gained a measure of nationwide prominence. The Kentucky Colonel had done everything President Sexton and the local supporters had hoped for. Centenary now had over 400 students, more professors and buildings, and a six-fold increase in endowment. A college on the brink of closing three years before had been saved, in part by its football team.

These had been happy years for Bo and Marie. A daughter, Fleurette, was born on 8 March 1923, and was promptly dubbed "Bo Peep." She became the delight of her parents. With a family to support, and a vague claim that Centre had sent him a large bill for something that he never explained, he had supplemented his income a few thousand dollars during the first two seasons by playing an occasional exhibition game and by signing with two teams of the newly formed and struggling National Football League.

He was on the roster of the Milwaukee Badgers for 1922 and the Cleveland Indians for 1923, but he could only play when his Centenary team had a game in the North on the Saturday before the professional game on Sunday. With the plays and signals mailed to him the week before, he would arrive at the stadium, collect his money in advance, and play without practice. Not trusting locker rooms, he was seen once to stuff his bills in his football pants. During the game a hard tackle split the moleskins, and the play had to be stopped while he picked up his money to the amusement of thousands of fans. In November 1922 he directed the Badgers against Jim Thorpe's Oorang Indians in Milwaukee after Centenary had played the day before in Louisville. More incredible, the next year he quarterbacked the Indians in Cleveland the Sunday after his team had lost in Boston on Saturday. This was apparently his last game in organized professional football, but the experience of playing briefly in the National Football League left him with the firm opinion that the college game was morally and physically superior to the professional. Nonetheless, his few games for pay helped to keep before the public the reputation of the man hailed by the *Cleveland Plain Dealer* in 1923 as the "greatest collegiate player of the last decade."

As much as he loved coaching, a shadow lay over McMillin's career. His fabulous success at Centre and Centenary had given rise to stories that these two small colleges freely violated academic standards to win football fame. Centre had played Harvard again in 1922 and, though losing, remained a nationally ranked team. The following year the Colonels met the University of Pennsylvania in Philadelphia before an even larger crowd than had seen them play in the Harvard Stadium. By the end of the 1923 season a hue and a cry against the alleged evils of college football could be heard from the faculties of many colleges across the nation, a cry echoed by the Chief Justice of the United States. If large universities had to bend the rules to recruit capable players, what must schools as small as Centre and Centenary be doing? In the South, these two colleges had become the institutional symbols of what many feared must lie in the shadow of college athletics, and by their recent conspicuousness Moran and McMillin had come to personify these supposed abuses. Even in Danville and Shreveport, some professors complained about the absence from class of football players away on long trips. Neither college had entirely clean hands. McMillin had played for Centre in 1921 while apparently ineligible, and in three years at Centenary Cal Hubbard had earned only thirty-two college credits. These two small colleges were hardly among the most flagrant violators of academic standards, but they were easy targets to be held up as bad examples.

Centenary had never been admitted to the Southern Association of Colleges and Secondary Schools, the accrediting body for the southern states. President Sexton was eager to climax the college renaissance by securing admission and thus full accreditation for Centenary's degrees. The executives of the association, however, expressed more concern over "a disproportionate emphasis on athletics" than over deficiencies in the library and science laboratories. McMillin's salary was particularly galling to the faculties of other southern colleges, and the inherent dangers of permitting people outside the institution, even gamblers in the worst case, to pay the coach were apparent. He agreed at first to coach another season at a lower figure, but Sexton received a clear message that letting Bo go would remove the last barrier to accreditation. His contract was not renewed, and Centenary became a member of the Association. As the student newspaper bluntly stated the relationship of these two events, "Such was the price of membership Centenary had to pay."

Centre College was likewise threatened. Although a member of the Southern Association, the college had been required to undergo a prolonged review during which larger institutions vented their jealousy of the football fame won by its teams. A committee of the Association charged that Centre's athletic department was corrupt, that it forced the admission of athletes unqualified for college, and that the college sought to gain from "unethical" publicity. Furthermore, the new president, R. Ames Montgomery, was told that the faculty at such an institution must be as "rotten as your athletics." Montgomery admitted that there had been "some slight irregularities" in the past, but provided evidence that several other southern schools were as guilty or more so. By the end of the 1923 season it became so obvious that the Association's animosity was directed toward Moran that he resigned in a huff, proclaiming that he would never again coach at a southern college even though the University of Alabama had offered him a position at a substantial increase over his salary at Centre.

With Moran gone, a demand arose from alumni, Kentucky fans, and even some trustees that Centre hire McMillin to coach. President Montgomery was caught in the middle, for he had been told that the Association would never approve a college that employed either McMillin or Moran. These men, he knew, were objectionable to the Association "in their professional character evidenced in the high salaries paid to them and in the character of their training and publicity." And he himself was stubbornly opposed to paying a coach more than the president. But he gave in to "a state all stirred up" and in January 1924 brought McMillin to Danville for a meeting, at which local trustees forced him to make an offer of $7,500—the president's salary after adding the value of his house — and $1,500 for "field service," apparently recruiting and fund raising. Centre's most famous son, however, flatly refused to accept the split salary or to give up whatever income from professional football he might make. Montgomery was much relieved when McMillin's acceptance of another offer relieved the president of the necessity of choosing between the college's accreditation and the support of trustees and alumni, perhaps even his job. With neither Moran or McMillin in its employ, Centre College was quickly approved by the Association.

McMillin appears to have taken the best position he could obtain outside the South where he had been blacklisted as a coach. He went to Geneva College in Beaver Falls, Pennsylvania, at a salary of only $7,500, although it was $3,500 more than the president's. But there were other inducements. Geneva, located in the heart of the Pennsylvania-Ohio border region noted for producing football players, was building a handsome new stadium and was eager to play big time football. Here was an ideal location from which to demonstrate his coaching skills to a wider circle. New to the area, he could expect additional income from the motivational talks for which he was becoming noted. And he may have received some assurances that his salary would be unofficially supplemented, for the Geneva alumni magazine referred to "certain individual alumni" who support the athletic program "generously and loyally." The college's rigid Sabbatarianism would prevent his playing professional games on Sunday, and thus give him more time to spend with his family. Whatever his financial arrangements, he was soon much at home in Beaver Falls.

Geneva College was sponsored by the Reformed Presbyterian Church of North America, a small body that carried on the Calvinistic traditions of the Scottish Covenanters. With an enrollment of over 400 day students and as many more in evening classes, this church college provided higher education for a significant proportion of the residents of the Beaver Valley, an industrial area north of Pittsburgh. Geneva officials knew of McMillin's fame as a member of the Praying Colonels and had read his explanation that after leaving Centre he had turned down more attractive offers because "[he] believed in the moral ideals for which Centenary College stood." With a name that could be Scottish, a reputation for piety and morality, and having come to fame at a Presbyterian college, he seemed ideal for Geneva.

Those who remember Bo McMillin's entrance into Beaver Falls still delight in telling that he drove to the campus in the only Cadillac in town and was taken to the home of a college official, Dr. Robert Clarke, for dinner. When grace was said before the meal, the new coach crossed himself. As the story goes, Dr. Clarke did not enjoy the remainder of his meal. He, like many of the Covenanters, was a staunch anti-Catholic as a result of his childhood experience in Northern Ireland. Apparently no one at Geneva had known that McMillin was Catholic.

Nonetheless, the Catholic Bo took Presbyterian Geneva by storm. He made the college officials proud when he told a press conference in Pittsburgh that he was a "God-fearing man" who would not "tolerate any shady tactics on the part of his team," play any man who received money for playing or was "down in his studies, or ever use a "ringer." (The administration did, however, provide tuition grants for football and basketball players.) With the hero of *First Down Kentucky* as its coach, Geneva promised to take the lead in cleaning up football in Western Pennsylvania. True to his word, he refused to break the rule that transfers must sit out a year for the three pillars of his Centenary team who had followed him to Geneva. As a result, Cal Hubbard, Osseo W. "Oz" Maddox, and Carl "Swede" Anderson — three men who could have started for almost any team in the country — did not play in 1925. Only one Centenary player, Mack Flenniken, a powerful fullback, got around the rule by attending Geneva a semester before the season began. The sight of Cal Hubbard, "the biggest man in Beaver Falls," giving up a year of football and supporting himself by waiting on tables and working weekends in a cork factory in order to be near his coach offered convincing testimony to the influence of Bo McMillin.

Except for his attending Mass, the new coach was everything the college could have wanted. He spent hours outside of practice counseling with his players and other students or simply enjoying games of chess or checkers with them in the dormitories or his home. Soon he was a featured speaker at the required chapel services, and he proclaimed his philosophy of life by having the student newspaper publish "Bill Jones" or "the Game of Life," as the poem was sometimes titled. The essence of Bo's philosophy was that successful athletics must be a by-product of character building. He pushed his players not only to study but to get involved in such activities as debate and glee club. On road trips he urged the team to attend church on Sunday, and he would sometimes attend Protestant services with them. And of course, there was prayer in the locker room before a game. Mrs. McMillin's southern hospitality and open-heartedness made her as popular with female students as he with the men. From the dormitory where the McMillins lived at first, Little "Bo Peep" toddled after "Daddy Bo" across the small campus and drew her own share of the affection poured out on this family. It is hardly surprising that the college administration diplomatically pushed aside the protests of a few Reformed Presbyterian churches that their college had hired a Catholic coach. But McMillin remained himself. One Geneva player vividly recalled being recruited for the team when he encountered the famous man showing his expertise with a cue stick in a Beaver Falls poolroom.

In the past Geneva football teams had held their own with colleges of similar size but had encountered disaster against major schools like West Virginia and nearby rival the University of Pittsburgh, which had now dropped the Covenanters team from its schedule after four successive drubbings. With his three Centenary players sitting out, McMillin managed to win six games while losing three in 1925. He used this season to introduce his system of football and to groom the men he would have the following year. The satisfaction of the Geneva community with its new coach swelled when in December he announced that his Gold and White team would open the 1926 season against the football giants, Cornell and Harvard. Don't worry, he told his boys, Ivy League gridiron stars "put on their pants one leg at a time, the same as we do."

Having scheduled Geneva as a "breather" to open the season, Cornell was fortunate to escape with a 6-0 win, made possible, so McMillin and his players believed, only because they were heavily penalized by biased officials. The next week's game in Cambridge drew national attention because it matched McMillin's team against the squad of the new Harvard coach, Arnold Horween, the captain of the Crimson against Centre in 1920. The game was never in doubt. With end Hubbard rolling up the Crimson line, fullback Flenniken ran for long gains. For the first time in its gridiron history, Harvard lost an opening game. Back in Beaver Falls the bell of Old Main rang out through the Valley the news to be proclaimed the next day in the headline of the *New York Times*: "Harvard Humbled by Geneva, 16-7." Coach Horween acknowledged after the game that this Geneva team was "one of the best trained elevens" ever to play in Harvard Stadium. Like Centre in 1921, Geneva's victory over Harvard in 1926 became a highlight of the college's history, a memory refreshed for decades to come each time a student or alumnus passed the game ball, displayed all alone in its handsome trophy case. For Colonel Bo, the nationwide publicity given this game marked his transformation in the public eye from star player to first-rate coach.

Only a fluke loss to Grove City College spoiled a perfect season for the Covenanters in 1926. Still Geneva was invited to its first post-season game, at the Orange Blossom Festival at Jacksonville, Florida, where the Covenanters defeated Oglethorpe University 9-7, a victory tarnished, according to the college authorities, by a too rowdy post-game celebration. Despite the success of his team, it had been a sad year for the coach. Marie McMillin had died of pneumonia in March, soon after their fourth wedding anniversary. Three-year-old Fleurette had also been near death but eventually recovered. An outpouring of sympathy and affection from the college and community testified to the esteem in which both husband and wife were held. Among those attending the funeral was Chief Myers. While in town he made "a very touching address to the student body" in which he praised his protégé as a man as well as a coach.

Cal Hubbard left at the end of the school year without graduating to play for the New York Giants of the National Football League, where his greatness was soon recognized. Red Grange, successor to Bo as the nation's most sensational player, described Hubbard as "the greatest tackle I've ever seen — or been pulverized by." After his outstanding football career, Hubbard entered baseball as an American League umpire. In 1976 he was voted into the Baseball Hall of Fame, the first man to be selected for the Hall of Fame in both baseball and professional football. Until his dying day, Hubbard gave the credit for his fabulous athletic career to his coach at Centenary and Geneva, who had "broken" a strong but wild young "horse."

Genéva went undefeated, though tied once, in the 1927 season. Yet this near perfect record may have seemed anticlimactic to McMillin. Except for a 13-0 win over Boston College in that city, the Covenanters had been able to schedule games only with regional schools. He had sought in vain to get Geneva invited to a post-season game in California. With a record of fifty-two wins, eight losses, and one tie in six years, he had nothing left to prove by coaching small college teams. At Geneva he was required to coach basketball and track at a time when football coaching was becoming a highly specialized, year-round profession. By the beginning of 1928 he needed a new challenge, one that would test whether his coaching style would be effective in a large college whose teams regularly played major opponents.

The Kansas State Agricultural College (later Kansas State University) provided that challenge. Located in Manhattan, 100 miles west of Kansas City, this land grant college enrolled some three thousand students and played in the Big Six Conference against Iowa State, Nebraska, Missouri, Oklahoma, and the University of Kansas. Although this conference did not yet get the publicity given the Ivy League and the Big Ten, the quality of its football and the intensity of the rivalry were hardly surpassed elsewhere. The previous coach, Charlie Bachman, had given Kansas State football respectability for the first time, including victories over intrastate rival Kansas. Yet Bachman, whose long career would result in one of the best winning percentages of all coaches of his era, had been unable to win the Big Six championship. Building a stadium in the 1920's and beginning to play big-time football were important parts of the college's quest for identity in the face of the greater visibility of the better known University of Kansas. No record of the salary offered McMillin has been found, but it is unlikely that he received much if any more than at Geneva. For him now, professional advancement was more important than money.

Colonel Bo found a congenial atmosphere among the 10,000 residents of the pleasant, park-like town of Manhattan in which his high standards of conduct were community norms. The moral revolution of the 1920's, of which Sigmund Freud was the "high priest" and D. H. Lawrence the "prophet," seemed largely to have missed the Kansas State campus, where President Francis D. Farrell stood guard against cigarettes, bootleg booze, and short skirts on Jazz Age flappers. A brief stay on the campus in March for spring football practice "was long enough," so the alumni magazine announced, "to give everybody in the community a pretty thorough knowledge of McMillin's code of ethics and sportsmanship." That fall, students took quickly to a coach who spent his leisure hours with them, "not as a driver or commander but as a pal." His support of other campus activities, his loud insistence that his players keep up their grades, and his extraordinary ability to capture an audience soon attracted a personal following among faculty and undergraduates that would survive even losing football seasons. After his team lost its opening game of 1928, the alumni magazine reported that, despite the defeat, "McMillin himself has scored a victory at the college, in that he has instilled a school spirit and a team spirit of the highest type."

At first, some of the returning players from the 1927 season did not take seriously their new mentor's rules. The former coach had been noted for his strong language, but McMillin quickly demonstrated that his ban on swearing was firm by benching his captain who let slip an oath during a game. His players never forget Bo's substitute expletives, such as "Oh, my achin' back!," "Oh, my side and body!," "I'll be a dirty name!," or "Well, I'll be a glass man!" Such expressions, with a boy's name attached, could sear forever the memory of one who had missed an assignment during a crucial game. But Coach Bo was quick to apologize when his emotional tension led to angry rebukes. During one game at Kansas State he ran to a player, jumped on him with hands around the neck and legs scissored around the body, and screamed, "Bill, I'm goin' to shoot you at sunrise." Bo's "pore lil' boys," for each of whom he had a pet name, soon realized the intensity that their coach demanded. His pre-game and half time locker room admonitions were unforgettable, although before one especially significant game he brought the entire squad to tears with "I have nothing to say." He took with him to Kansas State as line coach his Geneva tackle, Osseo Maddox, and in 1931 he employed another of his former players, "Swede" Anderson, to take charge of the freshman team. If McMillin had a major coaching weakness, it was his inability to delegate responsibility to assistants. Regardless of the number provided him at Kansas State, he remained a one-man coaching staff who, like Uncle Charlie Moran, personally supervised every detail of training. Thus he worked much better with former players, who still gave him a degree of worship, than with less awe-struck assistants who sometimes expressed discontent that at practices they stood around with little to do. As one of his assistant coaches recalled a half-century later, "he saw to everything himself."

Teaching a completely different system and depending heavily on freshmen, the new coach failed to win a single Big Six conference game in 1928 and finished with only three victories in eight games. Most heartbreaking was a 7-0 loss to the Kansas Jayhawks. For the first time in his football career, both as player and coach, Bo McMillin suffered a losing season. Undaunted, he set to work to build for the future. If he was going to produce a winner, he would have to use the material at hand and any high school player who might come to Kansas State because of the coach's fame. Athletic director "Honest Mike"

Ahearn was firmly opposed to giving athletes one cent of financial support beyond helping them find part-time jobs. On one occasion he promptly suspended the captain-elect who was caught receiving a salary for playing from a supporter of the team. Nearby schools were not always so pure. The University of Kansas drew a one-year suspension from the Big Six for covering up a similar violation, and the University of Iowa suffered a like penalty in the Big Ten. McMillin's professed football idealism fitted nicely with Ahearn's principles but proved a handicap in recruiting.

Bo's nephew, Ray McMillin, who had come to live with his uncle after the death of his father, became eligible for the team in 1929 and provided three years of outstanding play at quarterback. During spring practice 1929, McMillin saw a student kicking fifty-yard spirals and throwing long passes on the edge of the field. "Why aren't you out for football?" he demanded of the young man. Elden Auker replied that he wanted to play football but had been warned by a physician against ever playing again following a neck injury on a high school gridiron. Unwilling to waste such talent, McMillin arranged for medical treatment and physical therapy that enabled Auker to become a triple-threat backfield star for the next three seasons. Playing football contributed inadvertently to Auker's future success as a pitcher for the Detroit Tigers. After suffering a shoulder separation in a game against Purdue, he found that he could no longer pitch overhand or side arm, but could throw hard underhand, a style that brought him to fame in the 1934 and 1935 World Series.

McMillin discovered a few other notable players, including end Henry Cronkite, a first-team All-American in 1931, and Ralph Graham, three times All-Big Six Fullback. Yet generally he never had the size and depth of the best conference teams. Too many of his players were like Paul "Pete" Fairbank, who always treasured his coach's remark, "Fairbank, you have an All-American heart but a weak body." To compensate for what he lacked in material, McMillin resorted to tactical innovations that made even losing games more exciting and consternated opposing coaches. Most sensational was what became known as the the five-man backfield, a strategem made possible by the rule of this period that required the offensive team to come to a halt for only one second before snapping the ball. Five backs, three of whom started a step back of the line, shifted in and out of the line as signals were called, leaving the opposition uncertain of the formation and of the eligibility of pass receivers until a second before play began. Likewise, on defense Kansas State teams became known for the variety of their alignments against opponents that usually stuck to the old pattern of a seven-man defensive line.

After 3-5 seasons in 1928 and 1929, the next year McMillin's Wildcats finished third in the Big Six. The highlight of 1930 was a thrilling 10-9 win over Nebraska, the perennial Big Six champion, now coached by Dana X. Bible, who had become McMillin's nemesis ever since Centre's defeat by Texas A & M in 1921. In eight games as a player and coach against Bible's teams, this would be Bo's only victory. The 1931 season began with a notable 28-7 victory over the University of Pittsburgh. Then Kansas State compiled a 8-2 record, missing the conference championship only by narrow losses to Nebraska and Iowa State. Colonel Bo was now the toast of the campus. Imitating his drawl, the senior yearbook reported, "You all should know this heah 'Bo' McMillin from Kansas State. He's theah foo'ball coach. Yas suh!" His influence went beyond football. At one pep rally Bo told all of Kansas State's four thousand students that his door would always be open to any one of them needing help or advice.

The winning coach had other reasons to be contented in his Manhattan home. After sister Mina had at first kept house for him and helped to raise "Bo Peep," on 5 October 1930 he married Kathryn Gillihan of Gallatin, Missouri. They had met through a sorority friend while Kathryn had been a journalism student at Kansas State the year before. A son, Jere Robert, was born the following September, and a daughter, Kathryn Jane, in 1933. Hereafter, family life would rival football for first place in the life of husband and father.

In 1932 McMillin had to start over with a green team of mostly sophomores, but he managed a respectable record of 5-3. He rebuilt so well that in 1933 only a 9-0 loss to Bible's Nebraska Cornhuskers denied Kansas State the conference title. His veteran team was favored to reach that goal in 1934 in what had become, according to a historian of the college, the "enchanted age" of Kansas State football. But in the spring the campus and much of the state was rocked with the news that the beloved Bo McMillin had resigned to accept the head coach's position at Indiana University.

The Great Depression was taking its toll on higher education in the state. Enrollments at Kansas State had dropped by a thousand students, and the budget was to be cut by a quarter. Without details of McMillin's contracts it is impossible to know how these hard times affected his income, but it is probable that his salary was lowered along with that of other faculty and staff. Indiana's offer of a five-year contract at $7,500 would provide a safe haven in the Depression and would test his mettle as a coach in the Big Ten, increasingly considered the leading football conference of the nation. Furthermore, Indiana's customary position near or at the bottom of the Big Ten offered a challenge — another giant to slay — of the nature that the hero of *First Down Kentucky* had never been able to resist. At thirty-nine, McMillin seemed aware not only that he had a growing family to support but also that heroes do not endure forever. The sudden death three years before of Knute Rockne, whom Bo had idolized and held up as an example to his players, had left him deeply impressed with his own mortality. He might not have the time to wait for a more promising advancement than Indiana University could offer.

The team that Bo McMillin had built at Kansas State would win the Big Six title in 1934 without him on the sidelines, but no one could replace him in the hearts of his "pore lil' boys." After his players at Centenary, Geneva, and Kansas State had forgotten much about their gridiron days, the influence of their coach remained strong. When Cal Hubbard retired from professional football in 1936 and became an American League umpire, at games he often saw Elden Auker, whose pitching had helped the Detroit Tigers win league pennants in 1934 and 1935. Whenever they met, the big umpire was sooner or later certain to ask the hurler, "Do you think the ol' coach would be proud of us today?" It was a question that remained on the minds of many of the "pore lil' boys.

CHAPTER SIX

No Sexton for a Cemetery

(1934-1944)

Up to this time football coaches had come and gone at Indiana with great regularity and it had become a standard conference joke that after a man had coached there one season he accepted a road map as a part of his standard equipment.

Lyall Smith

Founded in 1820, Indiana University was one of the oldest universities west of the Alleghenies. So many of its distinguished alumni had headed other institutions of higher learning that the school had been dubbed "Mother of College Presidents." Its enlightened leaders had made it one of the first universities to admit women on an equal basis, to introduce an elective curriculum, and to offer military training on campus. From the time in 1917 that Bo McMillin had gone to visit his friend "Cow" Minton in Bloomington, he had known of Indiana University's long and proud tradition.

By 1934 the mixture of brick and native grey Indiana limestone buildings gave a look of tradition and unity to the 173 gently rolling acres of the Bloomington campus. Time had weathered and mellowed the appearance of many buildings that now seemed to merge with the tall trees and shaded walkways. Strolling through the lengthening shadows of this quiet campus at dusk, even the casual visitor could share in the emotions of "alma mater" that stirred the alumni who came back for homecoming each year. But that feeling of pride and nostalgia had seldom manifested itself inside the football stadium.

Not until 1886 had football come to IU, but that was long before the Big Ten Conference was formed, and long before most major colleges were involved in the game. Being an early adherent meant that many of the game's harshest lessons had to be learned the hard way. One account noted that the first twelve man football squad, captained by H. Wise, its fullback, went into their first game seemingly "unaware of the bruising body contact that would ensue," carrying "only one substitute, a sophomore named Ellis." The uncontrolled exuberance of the game quickly made it obvious that many more Ellises would be needed.

In 1891, another try at the sport came when Robert G. Miller, later a Bloomington attorney, arrived at IU to study law and brought a football. A team was organized and Billy Herod, of Indianapolis, came up to coach despite never having played the game himself, though he had seen it played in the East. The record was brief, only four losses. By 1893, twenty-three men were wearing the Cream and Crimson as they closed their season by losing to Purdue 64-0. Finally, in 1899, in recognition of the increasing interest in football as an inter-collegiate sport, Indiana sought admittance to the Western Conference.

Participation in this early conference contributed to the regularization of football at Indiana, and by 1904, its football program had a coach, James H. Horne, two full teams, and proudly displayed its first well-padded uniforms. (Also) Indiana's first All-American, Zora G. Clevenger, captained the team that year. "Clev" returned to the campus in 1924 as athletic director, and held the post for twenty-two years, endearing himself to countless thousands of students and faculty members.

In 1926 the university celebrated the opening of its new Memorial Stadium by defeating traditional rival Purdue, but for a decade thereafter Hoosier football fans found little else to cheer about. Their team finished persistently near or at the bottom of the Big Ten standings with never a promise or hope of a championship. For the three seasons before McMillin arrived, football had been coached by E. C. "Billy" Hayes, the respected and renowned track coach, who had undertaken the assignment as a favor to President William L. Bryan. Such casual attention to football by a Big Ten university dramatized the lack of emphasis placed on the sport at Bloomington.

Obviously, Bo McMillin came to Indiana University with his eyes wide open. His five-year contract, he believed, gave him the time necessary to treat the school's football ills. He lost little time in reaching

Bloomington. On Sunday afternoon, 11 March 1934, he stepped from the train to find a welcoming committee of three. No bands played, no crowds cheered; there was nothing in Bo's arrival at Indiana University that gave any intimation of the folk hero he was to become there.

Characteristically, he set to work at once. On Monday afternoon in the field house, a hopeful crowd of fifty young men, eager to get a look at their new coach, turned out for spring practice. Despite his penchant for seeking and accepting new challenges, as he looked out over this group, he must have been weighing the size of the problem he faced.

In a conference with some of the heavyweights of national football, he would coach at a school larger than Kansas State but much smaller than most of its Big Ten gridiron rivals. Indiana, with a student body of about 5,000, competed with schools like Michigan and Ohio State whose enrollments already reached 10,000 to 12,000. And apart from the disadvantage of size, the physical facilities for football in Bloomington left much to be desired. The Tenth Street Memorial Stadium — an open-ended concrete horseshoe, seating about 22,000 — although dedicated only nine years before, was already overshadowed by the huge complexes of other state universities. Such unfortunate comparisons could only hinder future recruiting. Finally, there was the problem of the university's attitude. Had the long history of mediocre football, of finishes at the bottom of the Big Ten, of inability to attract talented players, so damaged Indiana spirit and prospects that the program could not be revived? Faced with these problems, many coaches might have settled for merely a few more victories, at best finishing out of the cellar in the conference. But not Bo McMillin. He was a fighter who loved bucking the odds, and finally was going to do his battling in the premier conference.

The acknowledged preeminence of Big Ten football could be credited in part to the conference's impressive membership of ten large state and private universities, but as much or more to a long and successful competition that went back to its origin in 1895. In that year the presidents of Purdue, Michigan, Northwestern, Minnesota, Illinois, Wisconsin, and Chicago had met in an attempt to halt the practices that threatened the future of football. They were appalled not only at the unrestrained violence of players determined to win at any cost, but also at the lack of eligibility rules to prevent tramp athletes from drifting from school to school and playing without ever becoming legitimate students. In addition to seeking solutions to these problems, the presidents addressed parity in scheduling. From their deliberations in 1895 had emerged the Western Conference with a body of rules that established faculty control of the game. In time Iowa and Indiana were added, and finally, when Ohio State joined in 1912, the conference became the Big Ten. The Midwest's ten largest, most prestigious universities had created a conference that would dominate college football in the area and whose champion would be recognized among the country's best. No wonder Bo took pride in just being there.

The Tuesday evening following his arrival, McMillin was given a reception designed to transform the University's attitude about football. Over fifteen hundred students, alumni, and friends of the University packed Alumni Hall to welcome the new coach. "I" men, instructed to wear their letter sweaters, gave the crowd a crimson tint as everyone applauded the University band and joined varsity cheerleaders in rousing yells. The mounting excitement erupted in a five-minute ovation for Bo as he took his place on the stage among other notables. The President of the Indiana Union Board, Eugene Fletchall, read a letter from Indiana's governor Paul V. McNutt expressing regret at not being able to attend and congratulating the school on its new coach. President Bryan offered the official welcome of the University. Sherman Minton, counselor of the Public Service Commission — later U. S. Senator and associate justice of the Supreme Court — recalled his boyhood days in Texas as a friend of Bo, and praised him as a "leader of men," predicting "that high school boys would be attracted to Bloomington because...[he was] coach." Athletic director Zora Clevenger brought cheers from the crowd by describing Bo as "one of the greatest coaches in the country" and promising that "the university would back him 100 percent in all he proposed to do."

When Bo finally moved to the lectern, Indiana got its first taste of his characteristic confidence and "down home" humor. "I don't intend to become a sexton for any cemetery at Indiana University," he declared. He meant it; his only approach to football was to play to win. He added, "You'll see Indiana win some football games in the next few years or they'll take me out and put me under six feet of earth." Bo was in his element, exhorting, challenging football fans. His sincerity won his audience, and as the *Indianapolis Star* reported the following day,

"His affable Irish manner changed suddenly to an intense fighting spirit as he told the team he would expect it to play the game for all it was worth, both in the classroom and on the football field." No one left the hall that night without new hope that Indiana's football prospects were brighter.

But winning would not be easy, as Indiana's prior record testified. Since 1885 there had been but twelve winning seasons, and none since 1920. Its Big Ten record was no better as year after year it drifted along near the bottom of the standings. Even traditional rival Purdue had consistently defeated Indiana in recent years. It was a football program in shambles. But undaunted, Bo drawled, "I've seen sicker cats than Indiana get well."

He would need all his curative powers, for while the Indiana area had always been a strong supporter of basketball, the state had neglected football. In fact, basketball teams outnumbered football teams ten to one in Indiana high schools. His goal of producing a winning team would demand that Bo roam far and wide in his search for "the kind of boy who hunts bears with a switch." So he began what would become annual six-month tours of the Midwest banquet circuit, speaking to hundreds of high school athletes, parents and coaches, preaching football, spellbinding all with his charm, and selling Indiana University's prospects. His talent for recruiting soon began to make a difference. For example, one night at a football banquet in Bellevue, Kentucky, future Indiana All-American Bob Ravensberg, sitting with his father, heard McMillin give his inspirational talk. At its conclusion he turned to his dad and said, "That's the guy I want to play football under." This skill in conveying his determination and ethical approach to sports won many a distinguished player for Indiana's rosters. His appeals touched something responsive in boy and parent alike.

This "pied piper" quality was essential, for Indiana recruiting was done in strict compliance with the Intercollegiate Conference proscription of athletic scholarships, a rule not every Big Ten university honored. In the recent past, one school had been suspended for circumventions such as "giving athletes a share of the commissions on the sale of yearbooks, utiliz[ing] a businessmen's slush fund...and [refunding] tuition fees." True, to assist with room and board, Indiana University provided many of its athletes (as it did its other students) low-paying jobs which, in themselves, could scarcely have been considered a recruiting inducement. And even though it was not an intercollegiate requirement, Director Clevenger went beyond the scholarship constraint, ruling that IU athletes had to pass all their classes in order to be eligible for competition. Despite the rumors that sometimes surfaced elsewhere regarding his recruiting, McMillin not only adhered to the conference rule but, in addition, heartily supported the requirement of academic performance. His belief in education was as strong as his commitment to football.

Recruiting was a shared responsibility at most schools and usually an important activity of the alumni, but McMillin found little such help at Indiana. He was constantly exhorting the alumni to "ship, haul or drive those babies to Bloomington," but with this audience, strangely enough, his appeal was less effective. The alumni never really promoted recruiting as McMillin wanted, and a tension resulted as long as he was at Indiana; but he always seemed able to charm away the usual alumni rumblings each season with results that brought Indiana football respect where before there had been little.

The first year of any incoming football coach is a time of trial; Bo's 1934 season proved no exception. More closely watched by the administration, the players, and the fans than at any other time, not yet having developed the special player-coach relationship so necessary to a winning effort, and limited by the football talent he inherits, a new coach is quickly put on the rack of wins and losses. Fall practice opened 15 September when only forty men reported, even fewer than in the spring. Bo's intensive spring drilling probably had wilted the desire of the less motivated. With assistant coaches Ralph Graham, Clyde Smith, Billy Thom, and former head coach Billy Hayes, who had agreed to stay on, McMillin set to work.

On 29 September, when Indiana rushed onto the field at Memorial Stadium for its first game of the new season with non-conference opponent Ohio University, the home crowd cheered the visible evidence of change. Gone were the old crimson shirts and familiar khaki pants of the 1933 season. Instead, the Hoosiers displayed black satin pants and new jerseys in a lighter shade of red with black satin numerals replacing the plain white ones of last year. Bright red stockings and a newly designed helmet provided the finishing touches. By smartly accoutering his players, Bo hoped to symbolize the beginning of a new era in Indiana football.

Ohio University cooperated by losing 27-0. The student paper rhapsodized in its next issue: "Indiana, after two decades has a football team. Bo McMillin and his charges have traded the Western Conference doormat for a barbed wire barricade, and you can mark them down as serious troublemakers for the Big Ten favorites." This comment proved nearer the truth than the writer imagined, for the game had scarcely ended before Bo's confusing five-man backfield had created rumblings throughout the conference. Designed to bewilder opponents by having various linemen join the backfield players before the snap, this innovative play shattered defensive assignments and angered other coaches. Francis A. Schmidt, coach of the next week's opponent, Ohio State, joined the controversy by describing "McMillin's unorthodox style of football as the trickiest in the Big Ten." By the weekend the matter had gone to Big Ten Commissioner Major John L. Griffith for a decision. Bo expressed no concern, since his system had already been declared legal by the National Football Rules Committee, and he pointed out, "I used it twice against Purdue — in 1929 and 1932 — and neither Purdue's nor any other Big Ten officials questioned its legality." The controversy ended when Major Griffith telephoned McMillin to advise him that the unorthodox system was within the rules, prompting the Indiana coach to advise the Ohio State Buckeyes that they would see the formation in the Big Ten opener that weekend.

Events soon proved that it would take more than the five-man backfield to climb the ladder of the Big Ten. An unimpressed Ohio State team brought Indiana back to reality with a 33-0 drubbing. And things did not improve as the season wore on. A single touchdown against Temple in a tie was the only Indiana score in the next four games. Then a narrow win over Maryland, 17-14, led up to the final game of the season, the Old Oaken Bucket duel with Purdue. The odds had never looked longer.

Beating Purdue was a rite of passage for any Indiana coach and could salvage an otherwise disastrous season. The game stirred emotions in a way that only Indiana partisans could understand and brought on a level of undergraduate hijinks that almost overshadowed the game. At Indiana the centerpiece of pregame activities was the effigy symbolic of Purdue's football prowess, "ole Jawn Purdue," who lay in state attended by vigilant ROTC guards at the Union building awaiting the festivities of the weekend. "Bucket" pranks took ingenious forms. One year Purdue students awoke the morning before the game to find the Bloomington city limits sign planted in front of their executive building and watched helplessly as an Indiana pennant rippled from a well-greased flagpole. Purdue's annual answer to Indiana's "ole Jawn Purdue," was the derisively delicate "Miss Indiana," who lay on her bier in their union building all week, awaiting her funeral pyre at the pep rally the night before the game.

Indiana's pep rally in 1934 took place without Bo. He was sick abed with a heavy cold, hoping to be well enough to manage the Old Oaken Bucket game on Saturday. But hundreds of students and townspeople were there, responding with enthusiasm to the speeches and college yells. Climaxing all, the cortege of "ole Jawn Purdue," heralded by the wailing sirens of the hearse bearing his Orange and Black draped coffin, wound its way through long aisles of hat-doffed students to the mournful strains of the University band's funeral march. Dressed in long black robes, "Sam Sirois, '35, read the last rites over the deceased, declaring "Ole Jawn" to be the "foulest and vilest creature in the history of mankind." Then with due ceremony, Indiana's symbolic enemy was buried in a muddy grave in Jordan Field to the cheers of the crowd. Saturday's game, however, would decide whether so "foul a creature" would stay buried.

The task before Bo's Hoosiers looked insurmountable. Indiana had not won a Big Ten game all season, and had beaten Purdue but once in the last ten years. Though Purdue required no further incentive, its heavily favored team remained unbeaten in league play and needed only this win over Indiana to share the conference title with Minnesota. On the other hand, Bo's weary and battered Hoosiers faced the final game, as one article put it, "held together with tape and gauze." Nonetheless, he was his usual optimistic self as he told everyone, "We're not going up there for the glory of old Purdue."

The game's first quarter was scoreless as the teams battled back and forth, punting for position. But the Hoosiers scored twice in the second quarter and the half ended with a jubilant Indiana ahead of a disbelieving Purdue, 14-0. When a 26-yard field goal accounted for another three points in the third quarter, Purdue's disbelief turned into desperation. Benefitting from Indiana substitutions, Purdue did push over a lone touchdown in the last quarter, but it came too late. Bo's weary, underrated Hoosiers had pulled off what the papers described as "one of the season's most stunning upsets." A delirious Indiana took possession of "The Bucket" it had seen only once in the last ten years. In a burst of hubris, the *Indiana Alumni Quarterly* boasted, "Since A.N. ("Bo") McMillin came to Indiana University, the eyes of the nation have been focused on Bloomington." Undeniable testimony to this national prominence had come earlier in Bo's selection to speak by short wave radio to the men of Admiral Byrd's Expedition at Little America. The occasion had special significance for him since two of his former players, Jim Stewart from Geneva, and Paul Swann from Kansas State, were members of the expedition. As his first season closed, no one in Bloomington doubted that their new coach had made a difference.

While unremarkable in the win-loss columns, McMillin's early years at Indiana did show progress. The 1935 record of 4-3-1 was the first winning season since 1920, and was climaxed as a jubilant Indiana retained possession of the Old Oaken Bucket by again beating Purdue 7-0. Bo needed only point to his consecutive wins over Purdue to speak of success. The school could walk a little taller in the Big Ten, for now it was winning more games than it lost, and football heavyweights like Michigan and Ohio State no longer looked on IU as a breather. McMillin's innovative approach to the game and his field leadership had won the respect of his players and his opponents.

To McMillin, the essence of the game was planning and strategy: success depended more on intellect than brawn, and proper planning could turn average players into exceptional performers. He excelled in this phase of the game. An incorrigible innovator, his games were difficult to defend against, to which any Big Ten coach would readily testify. His novel five-man backfield confused and exasperated coaches of the Big Ten Conference until the rules committee of the conference later outlawed the formation. Undaunted, McMillin came back with his "cockeyed T," an unbalanced and variable formation that proved equally deceptive as it presented a strong and a weak side backfield to mislead an opponent's defense. And he had his line backers "red-dogging" (today more commonly called the "blitz", when line backers desert their normally defensive role and make an all-out offensive charge at the quarterback) before most coaches knew the meaning of the term.

In seeking to disconcert an opponent and destroy his concentration, McMillin went to almost any length. Once in an important game with Ohio State he ran a play where his offensive line lined up facing its own backfield, and only at the moment of the snap spun around to face the other team. The idea failed, but it demonstrated Bo's willingness to experiment, even with the most bizarre of plans. His unorthodoxy surfaced another time when he made the radical suggestion that "coaches join the huddle and call signals, insisting that the mental strain on the player-signal caller was too great.... [Besides,] the coach was blamed for bad strategy and might as well be directly responsible." The idea made sense to Bo, but to no one else.

Although planning and strategy were important in McMillin's drive for excellence, practice, repetition, and attention to detail were no less so. His former players attest to his exhaustive preparation for games. His intensity on the practice field drew excellence from mediocrity: he knew that perfectly executed plays by average players could compensate for a lack of virtuoso talent. A hard taskmaster who asked perfection, he imbued the same driving spirit in his players. The recollections of dozens of his players testify to the unrelenting intensity of the man as he sought their best, and earned their resolve to give him nothing less.

This intensity sometimes had its lighter side. One of his assistant coaches, Ralph Graham, described the preparation for an important game that simply had not been going well. The head coach's exasperation increased as the week passed. By Thursday he had reached the flash point as he worked to perfect an intricate offensive play. In Graham's words, "We had a little colored guard, J.C. 'Rooster' Coffee, built like a ton of bricks, with a big smile, and a great competitor who was running his tail off,...[but] was becoming exhausted. Finally, Bo had all he could take, and as the team came back into the huddle, he said, 'You boys might as well get used to it because we are going to stay out here and run this play until you are black in the face'. There was complete silence for a few moments and then our little colored guard, with his tongue hanging out, said, 'Well coach , I guess I can go in now.' " The tension broke and everyone, including Bo, collapsed in laughter.

In 1936 Bo turned in a record of 5-2-1, the best in years. Indiana could point with satisfaction to conference wins over Michigan, Iowa, and Chicago, and, after a hard-fought tie with old enemy Purdue, continued possession of the much-prized "Bucket." Football had become a sport to celebrate at Bloomington.

To no one's surprise, the University acted to strengthen ties with its winning coach. On 10 May 1937, the Board of Trustees tore up his earlier five-year contract and signed McMillin to a ten-year one, raising his salary from $8,000 to $9,500 over its term. In so hazardous a profession as football coach, the ten-year term of the contract was unheard-of. The improved contract attested to the value Indiana placed on the contribution of its charismatic coach to its athletic program, and included unwritten but grateful recognition of his two wins and a tie with Purdue. To one as security conscious as McMillin, the prospect of a ten-year arrangement must have brought a sense of contentment. He was well paid and working at a profession he loved, in a major university where he had recognition and position.

The month after receiving this new contract, McMillin reached another milestone. Although he never admitted it, his failure to graduate from college must surely have been a secret embarrassment as he demanded that his players maintain their academic standards. He had left Centre College thirty-five credits short of his degree. While at Kansas State he had begun taking courses, and he continued at Indiana despite the mounting pressures of coaching. Unlike his haphazard grades at Centre, his grades now were all A's and B's, even in such heavy classes as chemistry and the English novel. Perhaps his campus importance as coach helped. He had other help: Centre College may have been embarrassed that its most famous alumnus was not a graduate, for someone there now discovered that McMillin had never been given the academic credits granted a few others for service in World War I. As a result, at commencement in June 1937, Alvin Nugent McMillin was awarded the degree of bachelor of arts. His diploma answered those who had scoffed at his promise, made when he left Centre in 1922, that he would be back someday to graduate. Among those present to congratulate the new graduate was the man who had scouted Harvard for Centre in 1921, close friend and now governor of Kentucky, Albert "Happy" Chandler.

The 1937 season, a winning one again, brought a record of 5-3, with an acceptable third place finish in the conference, but the result was tarnished by the loss to Purdue before a disappointed home crowd. The Ohio State game had proved the bright spot of the season. Indiana had not beaten Ohio State since 1924 and prospects for ever doing it again seemed slim. Bo needed some way to break this gloomy tradition. He had always been a consummate artist at finding just the right method of inspiring his charges, of firing them up to exceptional performance. As a special treat the Friday night before the game, he introduced his longtime friend, "Happy" Chandler, to the team. At game time, Indiana ran onto the field with its tiny squad of thirty-one players, dwarfed by Ohio State's red army of eighty-five that filled the opposite sideline. Despite this imbalance, Indiana clung to a 0-0 tie when the team clumped wearily into the locker room at halftime. The coach failed to appear for his customary exhortation. Instead, Governor Chandler came in and gave a rousing, tub-thumping, tear-jerking speech to the team. The result was best expressed by Bob Haak: "We knocked the door down of the dressing room to get out and won the game for Bo, 10-0." Significantly, they won the game for Bo — not Indiana. Although McMillin had no degree in psychology, he was a consummate master of the science.

The respect and even affection Bo McMillin won from the boys he led resulted from far more than the dictatorial power of the typical coach. His total commitment to the sport and to personal involvement in his players' lives gave meaning and purpose to his authority. These young men saw their grey-haired coach, the heroic giant-killer from Centre College, now become a father figure, sharing the joy of victory and the bitterness of defeat. His inability to keep food down on game days, his hat-twisting, gum-chewing nervousness on the sidelines gave evidence of the same intensity he had displayed that day in 1921 when he stepped onto the gridiron in Harvard Stadium. He led by example, dressing in the same locker room with his players, eating every night with them at the training table, sharing their jokes and camaraderie. On practice days, he charged all over the field, his head in every huddle, his eyes following every play, yelling praise or constructive criticism. He exasperated his assistant coaches, as he moved from one practicing group to another, taking charge, while they simply stood aside and watched. He sparkled with spontaneity, designing and rede-

signing plays on the spot. His rebukes often took the form of nick-
names: "Rockfist" for the end who dropped a pass, or "Ironhead" for
the unfortunate back who forgot his assignment. The colorful epithets
amused rather than hurt as players sought to avoid them by performance. From the moment he appeared in his office at 7:00 a.m. each
day, he walked, talked, and breathed football. His commitment to
clean play was well known and admired, just as his proscription of
cursing caused surprise and respect. But beyond football, he dealt with
the personal problems of his athletes, one-to-one, encouraging them to
seek him out.

Unlike some coaches whose interest in their players' scholastic
standing ended with eligibility, Bo sincerely wanted a college education for his charges. Perhaps some of his intensity on the subject
sprang from his own lack of a degree on leaving Centre. He expected
the same effort from his players in the classroom that he demanded on
the football field, never losing sight of the main reason they were in
college. Once, defending football against an academician, he put his
case in homely but effective terms: "No man has ever become a great
doctor, a great lawyer, a great business man, or a great banker, because he was a great football player.... On the other hand, many great
lawyers, business men and bankers have starred on the football field."
He embraced other football axioms, to be sure, but this one voiced a
simple verity of his "faith."

An influential role model, McMillin projected character, whole-
someness, and dedication to the boys he touched. Among his former
players, man after man later referred to the enduring effect on their
lives of the value system exemplified in Bo. George Taliaferro, one of
Indiana's great All-Americans, later wrote, "All of us who had the
good fortune to play under him ... are better human beings.... I have
attempted to emulate 'Bo' in my relationships with others." Bob
Haak, another great one, put it, "His players idolized him as a leader
of men." Quarterback Lou Saban added, "Those of us who played for
him...are better people because of our association." Another said,
"The things he taught have been a part of my life." This talent for relating to his athletes was one of his great gifts. He was friend, confidant,
and father figure. From this relationship, perhaps more than as a
coach, Bo's stature at Indiana grew. The sociological effect over the
years of the hundreds of young men like these entering the business

world imbued with the spirit of Bo adds a dimension to his role as coach. The late thirties produced other collegiate coaches with better records perhaps, but none held in higher esteem by his players.

As strong and effective as his rapport with his players had become, in these early years McMillin suffered recurring difficulties with the alumni. By its very nature the coach-alumni relationship frequently results in annoying friction on many college campuses. It was the same at Indiana. In Bo's case a major part of the problem lay in his natural feistiness. Tom Miller, sports information director at one time during Bo's tenure, described him as a strong-minded person who, far from being intimidated by his alumni, was quick to object to any intrusion into his responsibilites. One commentator wrote that McMillin was at once "the most beloved and most criticized of any of Indiana's coaches.... There were few middle-of-the-roaders;...[Indiana people] were either 100 per cent McMillin backers or enemies," and that time after time his detractors were disarmed by his bouyant faith in coming success. But personalities aside, the test for any coach with his alumni is his won-lost record, and McMillin's was not that outstanding.

The annual banquet given by the Indiana Alumni Club often produced grumbling and rumors of firing in an atmosphere sometimes less than friendly, but Bo invariably rose to the occasion. In his speech to the club, his capacity for optimism and sheer ebullience came through and brought the initially hostile audience to his support. As Ralph Graham, a long time assistant coach under McMillin, wrote, "Believe me, every person in the room would give him a standing ovation at the completion of his speech. Not only that but they wanted to not only renew his contract but extend it." He often used his Texas humor to turn aside criticism with laughter. One story told of a time when, after losing to Purdue, he was being pressed by a disgruntled alumnus to explain why on the game's last play Indiana could not score with the ball on the three inch line. Sighed Bo, "Reckon the field was a little too long and too narrow." Only a personality as strong as this Texan's could successfully pacify the alumni at the end of a losing season. One sports writer called McMillin "the Tops" in football speechmaking and compared him to Rockne, saying, "If you have ever heard the late Knute Rockne deliver a banquet talk, then you'll have some idea of what McMillin is like, because Bo sounds more like the late Notre Dame idol than anyone I have ever heard." These spirited reviv-

als of alumni hopes became almost an annual trial which he accepted
as part of the price of the job.

Coaching made other demands, not least of which was the time this
husband and father had to devote to speaking engagements. Later,
when he was named the Football Writers Association "Man of the
Year," his wife, Kathryn, only half-jokingly described him as the
"Missing Man of the Year." Known never to avoid a speaking engage-
ment, his attendance at about 150 meetings a year, everything from
from ice-cream socials to high school gridiron banquets, seemed to
justify Kathryn's pointed sobriquet. These speaking tours were probably less a chore than they appear, for through them McMillin preached
his gospel of football, generating dreams with his soft sell on Indiana,
and touching the minds and hearts of future ballplayers. A gridiron
Billy Sunday, he sought converts to the religion of Indiana football. It
was more than work; it was a mission. Apart from the benefits to his
university and to the game of football, McMillin's countrywide
speechmaking brought him increasing national attention and reputation.

At the advent of the 1938 season, in an atmosphere of campus optimism born of the promise of the prior years, the *Alumni Quarterly*
crowed that "If there is any sport fan in the United States who is not
now familiar with the name of Bo McMillin, Indiana's head football
coach, and Indiana University football, he is a subject for Ripley."
This nationwide awareness of Bo, by reputation and through his speaking tours, received resounding confirmation when football fans all
over the nation, in the largest total vote ever cast in the poll, elected
him coach of the College All-Stars in their 1938 battle with the pro
champions, the Washington Redskins. Indiana's President, Herman
B. Wells, wired the university's congratulations to Bo at the Palmer
House in Chicago, saying, "Your selection assures for the fans a great
game of football on the night of August 31."

The College All-Stars-Redskins game was the kind of underdog
contest Bo relished, and he worked his magic. The All-Stars upset all
the forecasts by trouncing the champion Washington Redskins 28-16,
and the result confirmed a McMillin conviction that a boy will work
harder for glory than for money. He took pleasure in having Cecil Isbell, brilliant back of Purdue, on his side for a change. Some joked
that Isbell's years of great play against Indiana had accounted for most

of McMillin's shock of white hair. Isbell gave the All-Stars their first touchdown in the game with a twenty-four yard pass to Johnny Kovatch of Northwestern. Later Isbell would go on to coach Purdue and Kovatch would come as an assistant coach to Bo at Indiana.

Bo's auspicious beginning with the All Star win dissolved into a season of frustration as Indiana fell to 1-6-1 and ended with another loss to Purdue. The only consolation was that things could not get much worse.

Just as there was little to smile about in the 1938 season, one incident exemplified the problems that beset the Indiana coach that year. Despite his firm belief in his ability to judge football talent, Bo was not infallible. One of his assistant coaches, Ralph Graham, recalls the story of the early search for a punter for Indiana. McMillin sent Graham back to familiar Kansas territory to find one, and a close friend of Bo's directed him to a young fellow named Bob Briggs. After watching Briggs in practice, making certain he would fill the need, Graham recruited him to enroll at Indiana.

Briggs had a miserable spring practice and, unfortunately, ran into his coach's close attention to detail. McMillin always had a strong preference for the step-and-a-half punt as opposed to Briggs' two-step style. The clash of the boy's natural rhythm with an order to change turned a problem into disaster. In desperation Briggs withdrew from Indiana and transferred to Kansas State. To Bo's mind this seemed no great loss, for he advised his inquiring Kansas friend that "the boy couldn't kick a lick." Graham concluded the story by adding that two years later, in 1938, "Briggs kicked the hell out of Indiana with his phenomenal punting and was instrumental in whipping the Hoosiers by one touchdown." It little helped the pain of losing when his Kansas friend came to the locker room after the game and reminded Bo that the kid "couldn't kick a lick."

As the Indiana years marched on, by 1941 McMillin had become a fixture, a celebrity both on and off the campus. Despite a losing record, by sheer force of personality, he had won over the school. And no wonder, for few could deny that his national reputation had brought attention, and even more important, talented athletes, to Indiana.

The Selective Service draft began to intrude on Indiana football when only forty men reported for the first fall practice in 1941. The group included a major find, however, in freshman Peter Louis Pihos, a six-foot one-inch, 210 pound athlete whose muscular frame seemed designed for football. A father-son relationship quickly grew between "Big Pete" and his coach that would not end until the younger man helped to carry the older's casket to its final resting place. Pihos' natural athletic versatility first drew attention: he could do everything well wherever he played—halfback, fullback, or tight end. Bo recognized his own desire and commitment in Pete. When Pihos, who had been an "A" student at his Chicago high school, slumped academically during his freshman year at Indiana, McMillin called him in and delivered a stern lecture on the value of an education against the day when he would no longer be playing ball. On the field, under skillful coaching, Pete was named All-American as an end in 1943 and as a fullback in 1945. He was elected to the Hall of Fame in 1966 and remains one of the greatest all-time Indiana players. When Pihos entered professional football, McMillin handled the contract negotiations. And later, when Bo came to the Philadelphia Eagles as head coach, he welcomed the chance to again be the mentor of this young man for whom he had so much affection.

After December 1941, McMillin faced a new antagonist in World War II. He lost his "seed corn" of freshman players to the more powerful recruiters of the armed forces. As the manpower bite of the draft deepened, reserve strength became a coach's fond memory; nevertheless, Bo made the most of the talent he had. Despite the limitations of his small squads, Indiana's 1942 game statistics revealed the team's greatly improved offensive ability. After being out-scored by competition year after year, the 1942 season found IU's points totalling an astonishing 256 versus only 79 for its opponents. And the Hoosiers had posted a satisfying seven wins against three losses for the season.

The season had included a tough loss to Iowa, 13-14, that stirred one Indiana Board member into caustic criticism. He wrote, "As your game with Iowa progressed last Saturday, I got progressively madder....The loss of that game can definitely be attributed to your bad judgment. The boys played a splendid game and showed the effects of fine training, but the management of the personnel, which was your job, was not well done." The National Football Statistical Bureau gave a different appraisal when its rankings placed Indiana sixth in total offense in the nation. In another significant game, Indiana handed the Minnesota Gophers a 7-0 beating, the first time in ten years that team had been disgraced by a shutout on its home turf. Even worse, Indiana's win ruined Minnesota's bid for the Big Ten championship. The climactic windup of the season's seven wins came in the third straight victory over Purdue, a convincing 20-0 shutout. A muddy field kept Indiana on the ground, but proved no problem for its swift back, Hugh McKinnis, as he exploded for two touchdowns. This winning season represented a major achievement, for the military had drafted all but two lettermen and one reserve player from the previous season's squad. The list of varsity lost to the war kept growing: Billy Hillenbrand, Lou Saban, Howard Brown, Russell Deal, and Hugh McKinnis among others. Bo was succeeding, as one writer put it, with "teams... made up entirely of boys under eighteen and 4-F's."

McMillin faced 1943 with hope since he expected to be heavy with experienced sophomores and juniors, but in these uncertain times the armed forces had first call. The manpower shortage had become so serious that the Western Conference decided to allow the participation in intercollegiate competition of freshmen and transfers from other colleges especially those in uniform. To further ease the problem, even scholastic standards were waived. When Bo assembled his hopefuls that fall, he found that all but two of the forty-four young men before him were pink-cheeked freshmen. His dismay at the prospect of starting all over again was lessened by the presence of a multi-talented seventeen-year-old halfback, Bobby Hoernschemeyer. Assisted by a war-reduced coaching staff of Paul Harrell, John Kovatch, Billy Thom, and E.C. Hayes, Bo developed his attack around this youngster.

On a pleasant fall day, 18 September 1943, Indiana opened its season against Miami of Ohio in Memorial Stadium. The afternoon's excitement was muted by the grim reality of World War II. The official program reminded the gathering crowd that there was a bigger game, with higher stakes, being played elsewhere in the world. It listed 6,000 Hoosiers serving in the armed forces, and sadly noted that sixty of them already had been killed. The news made it difficult to get the afternoon's game in perspective as Indiana and Miami battled to a 7-7 tie.

Despite the break-even 1943 season record of 4-4-2, Hoosier fans drew encouragement from the win over Ohio State—only the third time in thirty years — an especially sweet victory since it came on the

Big Red's home field. Actually, the season record was better than expected, for unlike some competing schools, Indiana had no Armed Forces-sponsored educational program that enrolled military trainees who were already experienced football players. In a period of eased eligibility requirements this represented a real disadvantage.

Fall practice in 1944 opened with McMillin marshalling a squad composed of nine returning players and thirty-seven raw freshmen. Despite the drain of personnel to the armed forces, Indiana's freshmen had desire and they had Bo's unflagging optimism.

An oft-repeated story of that fall practice still brings chuckles. Hoernschemeyer, the brilliant back of the previous season, reported late because of his preparations to enter the Naval Academy. Bo was reluctant to put him directly into the varsity line-up and discourage the kids who had already won regular jobs, so "Hunchy" found himself scrimmaging with the second team and being battered back by the varsity. After recovering a varsity fumble near the scrubs' goal line Hoernschemeyer made an incredible twisting, stiff-arming, broken field run through the whole first team and raced ninety-eight yards for a touchdown.

Still concerned that his star back might be too impressed with himself, Bo commented, "Hunchy, you made several mistakes on that run."

"Oh," a puffing Hoernschemeyer asked, "What were they, sir?"

Bo launched into his deflating critique, "Well, when you moved around end, you should have straight-armed that halfback, instead of rolling your body away from him, then cut back and kept going straight ahead. And when you got down near the goal line, you should have cut sharply to fool those fellows who were chasing you."

"Yes, sir," Hunchy replied, "I can see where there were several things wrong with that run. But, coach — how was it for distance?" While the record doesn't say, even McMillin must have smiled at that one.

The combination of freshman enthusiasm and Bo's leadership proved enough to produce a 7-3 season record with wins over some strong rivals. Yet joy over a winning season was subdued with the sobering word that now 8,000 Hoosiers were serving in the armed forces, and 152 had been killed. The football field at Indiana University was never far from World War II.

With the end of the season, Bo hit the banquet trail like the Methodist circuit riders of the last century, holding "services," mesmerizing football followers with his soft drawl, boosting Indiana, and searching for that one player who might make the difference. His eloquence flowed from conviction and love of the sport. A realist in most things, he was a romanticist about football. More than a simple sport, to him it was noble combat, character-building in its gentlemanly sportsmanship. Even before the upset against Harvard, he had gloried in the long odds of the underdog role. It intensified effort and magnified victory. Characterizing his teams as "pore lil' boys," dramatizing his opponents' size and talents, he loved the David-Goliath imagery. He relished the expected victory and cherished the one against the odds. He was still writing his own legend.

Even though his coast-to-coast speaking campaign demanded so much of his time, he still found it possible to keep up a regular correspondence with some of his boys in the service. One of these, Kenneth Moeller, spent three years overseas and had regular letters from his coach "relating news of other players as well as his own personal family." McMillin's special touch had long arms and his concern was real. In the quiet nights of those war years, he must have dreamed of the day when these men would put down their guns to return wiser and tougher, ready to pick up a pigskin and play for Bo.

CHAPTER SEVEN

None will excel it

(1945)

We shall not soon forget the thrills, the excitement of every game of this undefeated season. This is one season which will be replayed wherever and whenever two or more followers of Indiana University get together. There will be other championship years, but never one like this, the first.

Gaarland Haas

The successful 1944 football season demonstrated that McMillin's eleven years of hard work at Indiana were finally bearing fruit. He had raised Indiana to respectability in Big Ten football, from a lightly held opponent to a strong competitor. Hoosiers, unaccustomed to the experience of winning seasons, looked to 1945 with enthusiasm, convinced that their silver-haired coach could do it again. And while talk of a championship seemed unrealistic, to the conqueror of Harvard, no mountain was too high to climb. Also, the obvious progress of IU football presented an opportunity for the coach to advance another concern: his own financial security.

Although McMillin's 1937 ten-year contract still had three years to run, that obligation did not deter him from seeking an improved one. In late November, Athletic Director Clevenger revealed to President Wells that Bo had received a professional team offer at double his university salary, with a suggested starting date of 1 January. Aware of the negotiating leverage the offer gave him, but concerned more with security and tenure and anxious to stay in Bloomington, a confident Bo proposed to Clevenger a ten-year commitment at his present salary ($9,500), with the proviso that at the contract's end, he could, at the university's option or his, "give up the head coaching position to become a professor in the Department of Physical Education for Men." His salary would then drop to "that of a professor at from $5,000 to $6,000 a year" until his retirement, with all the pension benefits of that rank.

Enthusiastically, and with President Wells' hearty approval, on 13 December 1944 the Board of Trustees appointed McMillin an associate professor of physical education with faculty rank and privileges at a salary of $5,000, and also named him head football coach at an additional salary of $4,500 for a term of ten years, effective 1 July 1945. His retirement pension would be based on the combined salaries.

The alacrity of the Board's agreement to these terms symbolized the hold its football coach had on the university. Its members recognized the important public relations benefits of McMillin's untiring circuit-riding of the nation's sport banquets and readily admitted that his undeniable charisma had immensely benefited Indiana's improving football program. The Board would entertain no possibility of losing him. Nevertheless, one member, less than pleased with the salary negotiations, wrote Wells, "Your memorandum with reference to the final round of the shadow boxing bout with Bo McMillin came this morning. I hope the Old Oaken Bucket (budget) does not spring a leak." Obviously, the settlement was not unanimously popular.

At McMillin's insistence, Wells wrote the president of the Board of Trustees, Judge Ora L. Wildermuth, asking him to sign the new contract as he had past ones, saying he thought Bo "will feel a little safer." The judge returned the signed contract with his scrawled note, "Since I bawl him out more than anyone else, perhaps, he may have reason for wanting my signature. But I love him." For the "pore boy" from Texas, life had never looked better. He had lifetime employment, respected academic ranking, and full retirement benefits. Football had been good to him.

The summer of prospecting by Professor McMillin ended with the onset of preparations for the coming football season, one which the forecasters felt promised little hope for Indiana. *New York Sun* writer George Trevor expressed the general attitude in his pre-season appraisal as he favored Ohio State, Minnesota, and Michigan as contenders for the Big Ten title and dismissed Indiana as a straggling also-ran. The chances of repeating the fine showing of 1944 had dimmed with the loss of All-American halfback Billy Hoernschemeyer to the Naval Academy and center John Tavener by graduation. Worse, there remained not a single senior on the squad, but McMillin enjoyed the unusual advantage of fourteen returning lettermen, his largest pool of seasoned players since the war started. Brightest prospect among the newcomers was a highly-rated black freshman from Gary, George Taliaferro, who was impressive with his hip-swinging, broken-field running during summer practice. Coach McMillin noted with satisfaction that the young man could also pass accurately and punt for distance. He seemed a rare find. Just before the season opened the team welcomed back from the services two of its 1942 stars, Russell Deal and John Kokos.

Although the war had ended, the problem of the draft continued to plague McMillin. His football squad included thirteen freshmen already registered with Selective Service and subject to call, along with four others who would reach eighteen in mid-season to become eligible for service as well. And that was not all, for of the remaining squad, twenty held 4-F classifications which could change from deferred to eligible. It was clear that Indiana's prospects depended on what Congress would do with the draft law when it reconvened in September.

McMillin's intensive preparation for the new season got help from an unexpected quarter. Since 1942 Indiana University had been operating under a war-caused trimester schedule; it now reverted to the more normal two semester school year. The change delayed the start of classes, allowing a badly needed extra two weeks of practice to ready the young squad for the tough season ahead. McMillin later credited Indiana's fast start to the luck of these two weeks of added practice without the distraction of classes. Thus, before it began, the 1945 football year was marked as a portentous one for Indiana. For its coach, it represented the beginning of his twenty-fourth season of coaching, his twelfth at IU, and the well-earned title of "dean" of the Big Ten coaches.

Indiana opened the 1945 football season in Ann Arbor against the Maize and Blue of Michigan before a partisan crowd eager to see no repetition of last year's loss to the Hoosiers. However, Wolverine supporters were doomed to disappointment as Indiana passed and ran to a 13-7 victory, only its fourth win in the forty-five year rivalry, and three of these had been by McMillin teams. The game had many bright spots. Long an exponent of single wing football, McMillin came up with his own version of a T-formation that fooled the Michigan defense time and again. Ben Raimondi, lost in mid-season the previous year with a broken arm, returned to action with a vengeance. His passing accounted for both IU touchdowns, the only scoring of the first half. A new star loomed to replace Hoernschemeyer in freshman Taliaferro, who rushed for over 100 yards. A surpisingly stubborn Indiana defense let Michigan get no farther than the thirty-five yard line during the whole first half, and in the game's dramatic final fifty seconds held them scoreless on the four-yard line.

Beating Michigan had meant overcoming a problem Indiana had not run into before. In 1941 the substitution rule was eased to permit unlimited player changes throughout the game. Michigan's coach, Fritz Crisler, used the liberalized rule in this game to employ separate platoons for offense and defense, thus throwing in a rested team every time the ball changed hands, a tactic that left a smaller squad like Indiana's at a serious disadvantage. Bo had fresh reason to describe his charges as "pore lil boys."

The *Detroit Free Press*, in an unusual admission to its Michigan loyalists, reported, "Bo McMillin's men outplayed the Wolverines from the start and only a mistake in judgment prevented them from blanking the Maize and Blue." When the article unwisely referred to Bo's "poor little boys," Fritz Crisler let it be known that he wanted to hear no more "expressions of grief over these tragic figures and in fact will refuse to meet Mr. McMillin socially or otherwise until their next contest is decided." Bo's posture of the abject underdog "had become a red flag in the Midwest," where talk had already begun that Indiana was "the team to watch in this year's Big Nine Football championship race." McMillin's "sick cat" had turned into a roaring tiger.

The following Monday he went to Indianapolis to give the Indiana University Club luncheon his annual assessment of IU's football prospects. The three hundred boosters assembled there heard a confident coach promise a "fine season," but at the same time caution that "we must wait until the night of 24 November to say whether we have a great team." There was no need to explain that the success of the entire season meant beating Purdue that afternoon. McMillin's confidence soared when two former players returning from army service — his old favorite and 1943 All-American end, Lieutenant Pete Pihos, and his star guard from 1942, Private First Class Howard Brown — appeared unexpectedly at the lunch. Both decorated veterans were on final furloughs, awaiting discharge. Bo had special reason to be proud of Pete: he had won a battlefield commission as a U.S. Army paratrooper. The enemy had found him as tough on the battlefield as he had always been on the football field.

The university lost no time enrolling Pihos and Brown, for by Friday, they were attending classes, and expected to be in uniform for Saturday's game with Northwestern. Although they might not start, Bo promised they would see action.

Indiana got a shock in Evanston the following Saturday; the green Northwestern team played "tough," as the players described it. Toward the end of the first quarter, a blocked punt, downed in the end zone, gave Northwestern seven points that threatened to be the only score. Battling to protect the slim lead, a hard-charging Wildcat line frustrated the Hoosier offense and held it scoreless. Desperate, trying every passing trick it knew, Indiana pushed to Northwestern's five-yard line in the closing minutes of the last period. With only a minute and a half left, Ben Raimondi passed in the flat to Pihos who dragged three struggling tacklers over the goal line to score. According to one report, a Wildcat player threw his headgear down in disgust, saying, "Well, I'll be damned — I've seen everything now. They've got Superman [Pete Pihos] bundled up in a football uniform." Charles Armstrong, a returned Air Force captain who also had just rejoined the squad that week, kicked the extra point for a disappointing, but game-saving 7-7 tie.

In the sobering aftermath of the tie, Bo was cheered by the return to his coaching staff of Lieutenant Carl R. (Swede) Anderson, his former backfield coach, and the news that Lieutenant Commander C. A. (Timmy) Temerario, his end coach and old friend, was being released from the Navy and would return midweek. Since 1942 the IU coach had lost not only most of his experienced players to the armed services, but equally damaging, the heart of his coaching staff. The stopgap solution had been to enlist coaches of other IU varsity sports to assist in the football program. Varsity baseball coach, Paul "Pooch" Harrell, assumed the backfield duties, and Billy Thom, the wrestling coach, the line. Though the arrangement kept Indiana from having to hire new football coaches for the duration, it placed an additional instructional burden on McMillin, a situation that may explain occasional criticisms that he ran a one man show. The addition of Anderson and Temerario meant that against the Illini, the coaching staff would be back at full strength for the first time since the 1941 season.

The 6 October game with Illinois threatened to repeat the scary Northwestern tie until in the third quarter the Hoosiers pushed over the lone touchdown. Indiana still remained undefeated in the Big Ten, but the margin of victory raised doubts.

The next week's Homecoming game with Nebraska was another story. The game was no contest. By halftime non-conference Nebraska was smothered, 27-0, and IU reserves took over in the second half, pushing the score to 54-14. McMillin took his team next to Iowa City and humbled the Iowa Hawkeyes 52-20 in a game even more one-sided than the score indicated. Indiana's third Big Ten victory kept it in what the papers called "a challenging position for the 1945 conference gridiron crown."

After the Hoosiers next won a low-scoring non-conference match with Tulsa University, the mid-week Associated Press nationwide poll of sports writers ranked Indiana a gratifying fifth behind Army, Notre Dame, Navy and Alabama. This unfamiliar attention, national ranking in football above all its old Big Ten rivals, fed the sweet dream of a conference title. IU's thus far undefeated record created a situation in Bloomington reminiscent of the baseball no-hitter when everyone avoids talking about it, afraid the spell will be broken.

An easy game with Cornell College of Mt. Vernon, Iowa, the first Saturday in November seemed to justify IU's national ranking among the nation's heavyweights. The lopsided score of 46-6 prompted the *New York Times* to express the surprise of many: "Apparently, while no one was looking Bo McMillin's 'pore little boys' from Indiana have sneaked into a position of contention for the Big Ten Championship, a title that has eluded them for the past forty-five years."

McMillin didn't depend on preparation alone to win ballgames, he indulged his superstitions as well. On the way to the Minnesota game the following week, sighting a white horse found him spitting in his palm and slapping his thumb thereon for luck. Although his superstitions seemed antithetical to his strong faith, a cautious Bo would ignore no possible assistance.

That Saturday a bright sun shone from a cloudless sky in ideal football weather as 41,400 shocked Minnesota fans watched their heroes trudge off the field at the final gun, bruised and battered, shut out 49-0. Early warning of the impending disaster came when Taliaferro stunned the Minnesota crowd by returning the opening kickoff ninety-four yards for a touchdown. Indiana's victory over the Gophers was only the third since their series began in 1906, and was the worst defeat ever handed them by anyone. Now only a non-conference tune-up game with Pittsburgh remained before the final conference battle with Purdue. Trying to contain the welling optimism that surged through the campus, McMillin cautioned, "It has been a hard road and there is still a hard road ahead. On the next two Saturdays we meet teams which are capable of beating most any team in the country. Therefore let's stop this championship talk and concentrate on winning these next two games. On the evening of Nov. 24 after the game with Purdue, it will be time enough to discuss titles."

A rain-soaked crowd of barely five thousand sat through another display of Indiana power as the Hoosiers conquered Pitt, 19-0. Despite the effect of weather, the *Indianapolis Star* wrote that "Bo McMillin's 12th team has proved itself the most powerful to come out of Bloomington in 59 years of play." With only the final game remaining, and the possibility of a title looming, excited Hoosier supporters began speculating on the various outcomes. If Michigan beat Ohio State, and if Indiana lost to Purdue, Michigan would win the title. Or, if Ohio beat Michigan and Indiana lost, Ohio would get the honor. But if IU beat Purdue, the title would belong to Indiana. McMillin could see it no other way.

In the worst of times, Indiana's annual game with Purdue generated the soaring hope that a poor season could still be redeemed; and in the best of times, as in 1945, it spawned a paradox of conflicting emotions — exuberant confidence in the prospects of a proven team, along with nagging worry in the knowledge of what was at risk. This season, of all seasons, Purdue was more than the traditional enemy; it was the last step in the heart-stopping march to a conference title. If the usual pre-game celebrations of the undergraduates seemed a little wilder, if old grads wandered the campus in bemused wonder, if the coaching staff grew more short-tempered as the week advanced, there was ample excuse. Indiana had never been in this position before; it was a maiden try.

The week's festivities went on in an atmosphere of mounting excitement. Lying in state in Indiana's Union Building, perennial enemy "Ole Jawn Purdue" seemed a more threatening symbol than ever, while at West Lafayette, Purdue's undergrads were again vilifying "Miss Indiana," the focus of their determination to topple IU on Saturday. The ritual burial of "Ole Jawn" on Tuesday night followed a noisy pep rally and parade made unusually boisterous by anticipation of tomorrow's Thanksgiving vacation. For its part, Purdue whipped up college spirit with a huge pep rally Friday night featuring the customary cremation of "Miss Indiana, convinced that somehow IU's title hopes would go up in the same smoke. The Purdue band and a trainload of lucky ticket-holding rooters planned to come to Bloomington to help make the wish come true.

Thanksgiving Day was a holiday for some, but for Coach McMillin's Hoosiers it meant another day of intensive practice. He worked on defense as much as offense, concentrating on stopping punt returns. As coaches ever have, he warned against over-confidence, telling his team he expected trouble with a fired-up Boilermaker eleven. He would be the last to admit it, but he had his own battle to fight with over-confidence. His lengthening list of seasoned players back from the services and available for Purdue now included Howard Brown, Pete Pihos, Russell Deal, Leroy Stovall, Alan Horn, Frank Ciolli, William Buchner, Charles Armstrong, and John Kokos. After the war years of patch and fill, the Hoosier coach was ready to field a talented team as hungry as he for all that awaited victory. In Lafayette, Coach Cecil Isbell, who had been so troublesome for McMillin as a Purdue player, worked on the Boilermakers' aerial offense, hoping his Bob DeMoss, leading passer in the Western Conference, and Bill Canfield, top receiver, could upset IU. Amused reporters reminded Isbell of his prediction, made several weeks before the season started, that Indiana would win the Big Ten title. His prophecy notwithstanding, he intended to do everything in his power to thwart it. One Lafayette sports writer captured the feeling: "Purdue wanted to win more than it wants to go to heaven when it dies."

On Saturday, 24 November 1945, a bright sun rose in a cloudless sky over Memorial Stadium. Workmen rolled back the heavy canvas protecting the playing field from the recent snow, readying it for the most important contest in Indiana's forty-six years in the Big Ten. Thousands of fans fought snow and ice-covered highways for hours to be on hand for the big event. The local paper mentioned that forty-two state troopers would be available to handle the heavy highway traffic. On the IU campus, excitement mounted, and the union building overflowed with former players, classmates, and old grads who back-slapped and greeted one another effusively. But beneath all the jollity ran an undercurrent of anxiety that intensified as game time approached. In recognition of national interest, the major radio networks, Mutual and NBC, were on hand to do the broadcast from Memorial Stadium. Bill Stern, the noted sportscaster, not only planned to call the game, but the night before had originated his regular Friday night sports show from local station WIRE and planned to interview the popular singer, Frank Sinatra. Excitement over Sinatra cooled, however, when the local girls discovered that his words would be coming from New York.

By adding temporary bleachers at the open end and folding chairs around the field, a record crowd of 27,000 squeezed into Memorial Stadium in happy anticipation. Indiana's band, "The Marching 100," whipped enthusiasm even higher as the crowd, bundled up against the cold, nervously awaited the kickoff. The tension exploded in thundering roars of approval as the teams ran on the field, and the noise never slackened after the kickoff.

A bitterly contested, but scoreless first half was more a test of strength on line plunges, for the over-anxious passing attacks of both teams proved inaccurate. The Boilermakers were threatening deep in Hoosier territory when Ravensberg intercepted a Purdue pass in front of his own goal line and thus prevented a score as the half ended.

The air in the Indiana locker room at halftime was heavy with disappointment. The white-haired coach was deeply concerned, even shocked, at his team's uncertain play against a team rated far below IU. Before speaking to the whole team, McMillin grabbed Pete Pihos by the hand and pulled him into a smaller room for a private pep talk. Then with a half-time speech that, although unrecorded, may have been his greatest, he sent his players onto the field inspired to a new level of performance.

A tense McMillin stalked the sidelines as the second half began. On the second possession, Indiana's Raimondi heaved a long pass to Taliaferro who took it to Purdue's one-yard line. Pihos plunged from there for the first score. Receiving the kickoff in the end zone, Purdue mistakenly tried to run it out, only to be downed on the six yard line. Kluszewski covered a Purdue fumble on the one, and moments later Pihos plunged for his second touchdown. Hoosier fans rocked the stadium with their cheers and breathed a littler easier as they resumed their seats. The fourth quarter again featured rushes rather than passes, until Indiana punched to Purdue's ten-yard line and passed to Kluszewski for another score. With just five minutes remaining, Raimondi made a long runback of an intercepted Boilermaker pass, and the pressure began to demoralize the Purdue defense. Two pass completions brought Indiana to Purdue's four, and from there on the third attempt, sophomore Louis Mihajlovich pulled down a pass in the end zone for the final score. There it ended, a wonderful 26-0, the worst beating the Boilermakers had ever suffered from Indiana. Game statistics revealed a Purdue badly outplayed, with its vaunted passing attack left in shambles. Indiana had won its first Big Ten Championship and had its first undefeated season.

Cascading like water from a broken dam, the happy crowd poured down onto the field, laughing, shouting, some rushing to pull down the goalposts, but most swarmed toward the coach who had led them through this unbelievable season. Assistant coach Johnny Kovatch, who had so much to do with molding Indiana's great line, hadn't moved from the bench, but sat there in the midst of milling players and fans, drained by the tension, and could only mutter, "Boy, am I tired." "Pooch" Harrell, who had seen his Hoosiers play for the first time that season, having always before been on the road scouting, was teary-eyed, too choked up to speak, and just hugged Bo. Exulting players raised their coach, his face tear-streaked, to their shoulders and pushed their way through the cheering throng to the locker room.

The locker room was pandemonium. To inquiring reporters Bo confessed, "This is the greatest thrill of my life...even bigger...than the day Centre beat Harvard." He added in a voice husky with emotion, "They're the greatest bunch of kids who ever lived." McMillin introduced his old mentor, Robert L. (Chief) Myers, who when asked, merely said, "I can't say much, boys; all I know is that I'm prouder of

Bo than anyone else in the world." A roomful of happy Hoosiers noisily agreed. Kenneth L. "Tug" Wilson, commissioner of the Big Ten Conference replied, "You bet," to the reporter asking whether he thought the best team had won the conference. President Wells added to the excitement when he crowded into the locker room and announced that classes were cancelled Monday and promised a convocation to honor the team later in the week.

When things had quieted a bit and the coach could get the floor, he told the team, "Boys, man and boy, I've been working at football for thirty-five years. I've had lots of thrills. I've had the good fortune of being on championship teams and coaching championship teams before. I've made long runs for touchdowns and had lots of thrills, but what you did today was the highlight of my playing and coaching career. You're not only champions, you're thoroughbreds." Finally, when the players had dressed and begun leaving the locker room, Bo's easy Texas way with words seemed to fail him. All he could get out was "Nice goin', boys" as he emotionally hugged each one. The bond of these moments would last a lifetime.

Congratulatory telegrams began pouring in not only from all over the country, but even from distant places like Manila and Shanghai. And Bloomington was small enough to note that their superstitious white-haired coach began the week by getting a haircut, his first since the season opened against Michigan. Later, during a speech in Newark, Ohio, he tried to brush off questions about his phobia against barbers, saying, "I ain't superstitious, I didn't have time and I just decided to let well enough alone." Those close to him knew better. The championship produced calls for a post season charity game between Indiana and Army, but a standing conference rule prohibiting such games quashed speculation. Nevertheless, even the thought of such a game was heady stuff for Indiana to consider.

The Monday holiday at the university proved a work day for Bo. He made a quick trip to Chicago to address the *Herald American* Quarterback Club there. Over seven hundred rapt luncheon guests heard McMillin attribute the championship game to the inspired play of his friend Pete Pihos, the ex-paratrooper with the five battle stars on his service ribbons. He made much of the maturity of the returning servicemen and the leadership they contributed to the team.

The Boston American edition of Oct. 29, 1921 carries banner headlines about the Centre defeat of Harvard. Note the other news of the day is subordinated to the game. Inset shows Bo McMillin on the final dash for the only score of the game.

Quarterback McMillin shakes last Harvard defender on his run for the winning touchdown.

Tom Bartlett misses the extra point but Centre wins 6-0.

The triple threat quarterback.

1921, the team returns to Danville. (1) Bo McMillin; (2) Herb Covington; (3) Norris Armstrong; (5) Ben Cregor; (8) Hope Hudgins; (10) Hennie Lemon; (12) Buck Jones; (13) Ed Kubale; (14) Major George Chinn; (15) Terry Snowday; (17) John "Hump" Tanner; (18) Jim Priest; (20) Dick Gibson. Others: (6) Chief Myers (behind the wheel); (7) Coach "Uncle" Charley Moran; (11) Line Coach Tiny Thornhill; (9) Frank Rubarts; (16) Tom Bartlett; (4) Bill James and (19) Dewey Kimbell.

And the 1961 Reunion

Action at the modest Centre stadium in Danville, which remains much the same today. There are no face masks here.

*Left:
"Red" Roberts powerful lineman who also made All-American with Bo.*

*Right:
John Sherman Cooper later to become Ambassador to India and U.S. Senator from Kentucky.*

In the first Cotton Bowl, Centre fails to score by six inches against Texas A&M.

Cal Hubbard who played for Bo at Geneva College when they defeated Harvard in 1927. Later a great star for the N.Y. Giants.

Mel Hein another Geneva player who went on to fame with the Giants. "Among the game's cleanest players."

Bo as head football coach at IU with his staff.

All-American Billy Hillenbrand leads Indiana as one of its best players.

Always a part of the game, Bo emotes from the sidelines.

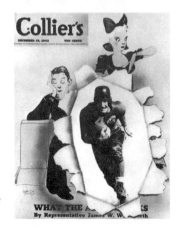

Hillenbrand on the cover of Colliers.

George Taliaferro one of Indiana's
great backs in the 40's.

Pete Pihos, another workhorse back of
Indiana fame.

Hillenbrand scoring against T.C.U.

A master speaker and raconteur, Bo appears before an Indiana audience in the 1945 Big Ten championship year, shortly before he left for the Detroit Lions.

The culminating event for the university came on Thursday evening at the victory convocation honoring the champions of the Big Ten Conference. Over three thousand students and faculty hurried to the auditorium to hear a parade of speakers celebrate Indiana's victorious coach and team. Standing before a center display of the Old Oaken Bucket, flanked by stern-faced ROTC guards, President Wells began by expressing what everyone felt: "Teams in the future may equal this team ... but none will excel it." Athletic Director Clevenger added, "It has happened. A lot of us thought we would never see it in our lifetime, but it has happened." Dr. Breneman, of the Faculty Athletic Committee, reminded all of the abiding interest with which the faculty had followed IU sports throughout its undistingished history in the Big Ten, and he concluded by noting that three of the faculty had "waited all of the 46 long years to see this day of glory." Roy Pike, honored alumnus and a member of the team that first entered Western Conference competition back in 1899, extolled, "A championship team could not have been produced without a fine coach and fine assistants. In Bo McMillin, our lifetime coach, we know we have the best....Bo, your 'poor little boys' have grown up."

Finally, President Wells introduced the speaker all had come to hear:

> Our coach is unexcelled as a master teacher of football — but that is not all. He is the devoted servant of this institution, its extraordinary ambassador of good will, an inspiration to changing generations of Indiana men and women, a Christian gentleman, and a leader of men. I give you the All-American coach of the year, and our coach of the year every year, Bo McMillin.

When the echoes of the thunderous applause finally faded into an expectant hush, Bo rose to the occasion with a captivating mixture of triumph and humility. He was at his after-dinner speaking best. He spread the credit around freely, and in conclusion, returned to the oft-repeated theme of his coaching career, a recognition that football was only a game, but through it the bigger, the vital, contest to be won was life:

> I sincerely hope that the championship will be an inspiration to every man of the squad and to every student. I hope the championship will make better men, better scholars, students

better in every way possible, eager to be outstanding and to live up to their full capacities. It would be a great source of satisfaction to me to think that the championship will not only thrill you but will make you get down to business. Not for my sake, but for yours. What you become in six years from now is what we're trying to build now.

The applause that followed made it plain that this white-haired football phenomenon, this drawling Texan, now and perhaps forever, "owned" this small part of Indiana.

In the days ahead, a round of banquets honored the team. Everyone wanted to be part of the victory. The Bloomington merchants and the Chamber of Commerce sponsored a banquet in the R.C.A. cafeteria and presented team members with certificates for gold Elgin watches. Then the University banquet followed at the Union Building with each letterman receiving a gold football with diamonds and rubies set in the "I." Later the Indiana University Club held a victory dinner for 600 alumni at the Indianapolis Athletic Club to honor the coach and team and to present each team member with a fourteen karat gold watch chain and penknife.

The frantic schedule of speeches and banquet dates subsided for the team but continued for Bo. He was off again on yet another series of speaking commitments in search of "boys who could hunt bears with a switch." The frequency of his speaking tours made almost believable a *Colliers'* article that quoted his wife's instruction to her children: "This is your father. Look at him well and try to remember the face. He is going out talking to the boys." Bo was fortunate that she knew the dream that drove him: the belief that football could redeem other boys as it had once done for a tough and cocky Texas youngster.

Awards were showered on the coach of the 1945 Big Ten Champions. First, the Football Writers Association of America voted him Football's Man of the Year. Then, after the results were in from a poll of 155 coaches around the country, in December McMillin flew to Bear Mountain, New York, to be named the *New York World Telegram's* Football Coach of the Year. The honor had special significance since his nearest competitor had been Earl "Red" Blaik, mentor of the great Army team, number one in the nation. At an interview later that evening, the old legend of his earlier heroics surfaced again when Bo said, "These honors make me feel just as good as the day I scored that touchdown against Harvard. Then I had to worry about Harvard coming back to tie or beat us, but I guess I got these for sure and can quit worrying." Every event, every success, was measured against the legend.

The popular magazine, *Life*, recognized his national prominence with a picture essay, capturing his hand-wringing, hat-crunching, bench-hopping intensity at the final Purdue game. And in the midst of all this attention a bit of commercialism crept in. A large ad of General Mills featured "Bo McMillin, Coach of the Year 1945," explaining that he ate Wheaties "nearly" every morning. Although well paid for the advertisement, his innate honesty must have forced the qualifier, "nearly." This endorsement later set off an extended debate over its propriety. Fritz Crisler of Michigan protested, "I think we should ban the endorsement of breakfast food. It's beneath the dignity of a [Big Ten] coach." An incensed and stubborn McMillin rejoined, "I have four kids. They like those things. If they are good enough for my kids, they are good enough for me. I'm going to keep right on signing the testimonials." And the fee for doing so was not unwelcome.

As expected, the championship brought plenty of All-American honors. Bob Ravensberg won nominations on six different teams, Pete Pihos on five, George Taliaferro on four, with Howard Brown and Russell Deal on one each. Howard Brown was named Most Valuable Player in the Big Ten, while Pihos, Taliaferro, Ravensberg, and Kluszewski made the All Big Ten first team. Even the university shared the spotlight as the nation's sports writers rated Indiana fourth behind the great teams of Army, Navy, and Alabama. Elated Hoosiers breathed the intoxicating air of national football fame after forty-six years of nondescript performance. Yet, despite all these encomiums, a disgruntled McMillin took umbrage that even more of his "pore boys" had not been honored.

It had been a glorious year, from the opening win over Michigan to the climactic victory over Purdue. Bo's accomplishment loomed the larger when viewed in the perspective of his difficulties. Through four war years he had endured the loss of coaches and seasoned players to the services, and wearied along with raw recruits, freshmen, and 4-F's. A greater problem had been the absence of an Armed Services Training Program on Indiana's campus. The record indicates that a limited ASTP program operated from 1942 to 1943, but nothing on the scale of larger schools like Michigan, Ohio State, and even smaller Purdue. To these schools a stream of experienced football players, now servicemen, returned under liberalized conference rules to resume college play. Despite this talent disadvantage, IU showed gradual improvement in the conference each war year, culminating in the Championship of 1945. Undeniably, the catalyst for Indiana's success had been the determination, drive, and charisma of this football wonder, Bo McMillin. His sheer joy in the game, love of a challenge, technical ingenuity, and innate ability to communicate with his "pore lil' boys" turned mediocrity into greatness and made dreams come true.

A few future detractors of McMillin would maintain that Indiana's only Big Ten championship owed more to the luck of releases from the military and the distortions of the war on college football than to the skill of the coach. But no such thoughts dampened the joy in Bloomington in the late fall of 1945. The fabulous McMillin had led the University from doormat to champion, had done what no one had been able to do before. Whatever victories Hoosier football teams might earn in future years, it was inconceivable to many, including President Wells, that any could excel the thrill of 1945. Nor could they conceive of a coach more deserving of the honors being heaped upon him. Indiana football history had been made and McMillin would be forever a part of it.

CHAPTER EIGHT

Where Will We Get Another Like Bo?

(1946-1948)

Bo was one of the few college coaches who didn't have to win to hold his job. Year after year Indiana trailed the conference pack, but when the Hoosier University signed up Bo in his last contract it was for 10 years. Indiana would just have soon made it for life. That's what Indiana thought of Col. Alvin Nugent ("Bo") McMillin, who had re-written Indiana's favorite song—

"Oh the moon is shining fair along the Wabash
Can you blame us if we make a lot of noise?
Through the sycamores the candlelights are gleaming,
For my po' little Indiana boys."

Grantland Rice

The emotional high of winning the Big Ten Conference title persisted into the new year, fed by the coast-to-coast banquet circuit McMillin travelled. He was the hero again, feted, lionized, and as always, a popular, peripatetic football propagandist who had lost none of his touch at the podium. One sports writer marveled, "People who can't stand banquet food go to banquets night after night, just to hear McMillin." Another described him as "a composite of William Jennings Bryant [sic] and Archie of Duffy's Tavern." In one of his more memorable speaking engagements, he addressed eight hundred members of the Indianapolis Ancient Order of Hibernians at their St. Patrick's Day breakfast. Amid decorative shamrocks, the sound of Irish airs, and talk filled with blarney, Bo was completely at home as he regaled his audience with "a choice assortment of Irish jokes, touched up with his Texas Panhandle brogue."

Indiana's newly won football fame together with a flood of returning servicemen swelled the enrollment in Bloomington to a record 6,136 at the first of 1946 and to an undreamed of 10,245 that fall. The Hoosier coach's obvious contribution to this harvest of students even led one enterprising insurance agent to propose that the university insure his life. The proposal explained that Bo McMillin "is to Indiana University's athletic program what Walter P. Chrysler is to the Chrysler Corporation.... McMillin has proved to be a master salesman for the University. He has advertised and been advertised widely. Thousands of dollars of advertising and future gate receipts will be scrapped at once if McMillin dies during his ten year contract."

So it seemed to many. With four home games to be played in Memorial Stadium, the advance season ticket sales for 1946 set a new record, and the local newspaper filled its sport pages with feature articles on returning veterans from the championship squad. But instead of writing an insurance policy on the coach, President Wells persuaded the Board to raise his salary to $12,000 for 1946-1947, the second year of his contract. McMillin's salary and faculty may have rankled a few, particularly as he continued to supplement his income with speaking engagements and a summer coaching school. For example, the controller of the university refused McMillin's request to keep his raise a secret, complaining that "people should know that we have a coach who does not regard a contract as a contract." However, in the bright outlook for the 1946 season, little grumbling found an ear.

Hoosier devotees were delighted when again a nationwide vote by football fans selected Bo to coach the College All-Stars in their annual exhibition game at Chicago against the champions of the National Football League, the Los Angeles Rams. To the national press covering the event, a cagey Bo protested loudly that his collection of college stars had no chance, after only three weeks of practice, against the professional champion that had played together as a team for years. On the night of the game, the ninety-seven thousand in Soldiers Field quickly realized that he had taken in everyone with another underdog ploy, the art of which he had first mastered in his days at Centre. By constantly shifting the positions of his defensive players, he held the Ram offense to only sixty-one yards. With the victory he became the first collegiate coach to twice win this celebrated annual game, as his national reputation and value to Indiana University soared. Hurrying back to Bloomington to coach his own team, he carried with him a low opinion of the quality of play in the National Football League, a judgment that would boomerang on him in two more seasons.

Back on his practice field, another matter divided his attention. Indiana's respected athletic director, Zora Clevenger, who had served his alma mater for twenty-three years in the post, decided to retire, taking a leave of absence until his official departure on 1 July, his leaving timed to permit the easy ascension of his friend Bo to the job. The unexpected announcement triggered a spate of endorsements of Bo but also raised serious questions concerning his qualifications. Bo lost no time in expressing his keen interest in the job to President Wells, certain that he could handle it along with his first love, coaching.

The coach's interest in the athletic director's position created a problem for the Board of Trustees, one not easily resolved. By 1946, the management of collegiate athletics had considerably increased in scope and complexity. Interest and attendance had grown markedly not only at Indiana but throughout the Big Ten Conference, where Saturday afternoon college football had become an important weekend social rite and a vital source of income supporting the entire athletic program. As evidence of its increasing popularity, football at Indiana was attracting a level of interest once reserved for basketball alone. In such a context, it seemed obvious that if IU intended to move forward with the times, the job of running its growing multi-sport athletic program demanded an efficient administrator, one of vision and capacity.

A sharply divided Board discussed Bo's suitability, focusing on the main area of concern, his lack of administrative skills. A few members pointed to his impatience with the paper work required in his present job and charged that assistant coaches now carried this load for him. As the Board pursued the question, several other candidates were briefly considered, but discussion invariably returned to Bo. The Board had not wrestled with this problem in a vacuum. Newspapers around the state strongly supported Bo's elevation as alumni groups joined the flood of advice and pelted the Board with opinions. The pressure mounted as a rumor circulated that, at the urging of Bo's old friend, "Happy" Chandler, the University of Kentucky had made an attractive offer to the Indiana coach at the close of last season. McMillin just laughed off inquiries about it, but the report was an unsettling element adding urgency to the Board's deliberations.

Unwilling to lose his coaching skills, yet wary of saddling him with dual responsibilities, the Board struggled for a solution that both met the university's future needs and satisfied those of their star coach. Although his national prominence and his admitted contribution to the college program weighed heavily in his favor, some members continued to object strongly to the impracticality of McMillin holding both jobs. At last, compromise came as discussion moved slowly in the direction of making him athletic director as well as coach, with the quid pro quo that a strong assistant director would have to be simultaneously appointed to handle the administrative work of the job.

On the afternoon of 23 September, the compromise agreed to, Wells phoned to advise Bo of his promotion with its accompanying $1500 raise, asking him to come at once to the Board meeting to settle the companion post of assistant athletic director. Still in football togs, he came from the practice field to the boardroom to formally accept and listened to the opening discussion on possible assistant candidates. The Board recommended Paul "Pooch" Harrell as an able assistant, but McMillin demurred, indicating his preliminary interest in Robert A. Cook, then publicity director. The matter rested there in deference to the new athletic director's wish to have an opportunity to think the matter through before deciding. Shortly after, the Board complied with McMillin's choice and appointed Cook to the assistant director's post.

For the superstitious, and McMillin was very much so, the jinx of beginning his thirteenth Indiana season made the possibility of duplicating last year's success even more uncertain. His worst fears were realized when first Cincinnati, then Michigan whipped the Hoosiers. In the weeks that followed, a struggling McMillin managed to turn things around by beating Minnesota and Illinois. But the reversal of form was brief; Indiana suffered humiliation again before a disbelieving home crowd when Iowa (the same team IU crushed last year 52-20) won in a 13-0 shutout.

Where was the magic of last season? The desire, the fight, the strategy were the same, but the magic blend of luck and opportunity that had made it all work in 1945 was gone. The rush to the mountain top had been an unforgettable experience for the silver-haired mentor, and the slide back down an unsettling one. Yet, though the 6-3 third place conference finish wasn't 1945, it was another winning season.

As he looked to the 1947 season, McMillin had greater cause for optimism than usual. His great running tailback Taliaferro and end Bob Ravensberg were back from the army now, and he could count thirty-three lettermen, mostly former reserves, in his squad of fifty who reported for pre-season practice. Also the presence of varsity veterans from the '45 and '46 seasons like Howard Brown, John Goldsberry, Lou Mihajlovich, Mel Groomes, and Dick Deranek added a wealth of experience and stability to the squad and brightened prospects considerably. The coach's one dark spot was the loss by graduation of his friend Big Pete Pihos, star fullback. There could be no replacement for him at the position, nor in Bo's care and concern.

The season opener at Nebraska wound up a satisfying win, 17-0, with Taliaferro and Harry Jagade starring in the eighth victory in the dozen years of competition with the Cornhuskers. A tie with Wisconsin, a tough loss to Iowa, and an expected big win over Pittsburgh preceded a disappointing loss to Northwestern, 6-7. On 28 October, the Ohio State game brought some measure of credibility to the season when Indiana hung on for a 7-0 victory. But the following Saturday, as it had last season, a powerful Michigan team completely dominated Indiana in a 35-0 rout. The season's windup with Purdue played to a victory hungry home crowd cheering the Hoosiers to a narrow 16-14 win. The game had some heart-stopping moments. One came when Purdue's only blocked punt of the season led to Dick Deranek's plunge for Indiana's first touchdown. Another came when, flush with a 16-0 lead, Bo sent in what he called "future hopefuls" and watched the lead drop to two points. Then during the final moments, in a sentimental gesture, he sent in all of his seniors to play together for the first time all season and their last time for Indiana. It is doubtful that Bo realized it was his last game, too.

During frequent post season absences from campus for his many speaking commitments, McMillin was approached in telephone discussions by the Detroit Lions of the National Football League about the possibility of coaching there. Amid much uncertainty in Bloomington over what was afoot, the rumors led the student newspaper to speculate that he might be leaving Indiana.

It would be easy to conclude that after the emotional high of a championship year, the now slumping football fortunes of Indiana had dulled the glow of Bo's fourteen years there, that the daily irritations had multiplied and his restless urge for new challenge returned. Perhaps he felt that the comfortable routine of college ball no longer satisfied. The reported tentative coaching offers from Kansas, Nebraska, and even prestigious Yale, had sparked no interest. On the other hand, he could not help noticing that professional football, after languishing behind college ball in public interest for years, was slowly finding its place as a major spectator sport. New coaching careers there were flourishing and reputations being made. Bo could see himself performing on a new stage. Besides, the needs of a young and growing family reminded him that the professional game now meant gold, and no one had to teach him the value of a dollar.

Leaving the warm personal relationships and the long term contract he enjoyed at Indiana would not be easy, but in some quarters evidence had surfaced of subtle changes in attitudes toward McMillin. Annoying rumbles of discontent over Bo's ceaseless speaking engagements that took him off campus so much caused some to call him not the "Graying Colonel" but the "Straying Colonel." Then, too, Indiana's 1947 season, a mediocre sixth place conference finish with two wins and three losses, had tarnished his image a bit. Alluding to rising alumni discontent, one wrote, "The wolves were howling...and had it not been for the upset win against Purdue, which was purely luck and no credit to his work or coaching, they would have besieged...the Trustees for his dismissal." All in all, his situation seemed ripe for change.

The NFL's Detroit Lions had just undergone a change of ownership. Fred Mandel, the Chicago department store executive, sold the team for $165,000 to a newly formed syndicate of Detroit business men and professional leaders headed by Lyle Fife as president. It was generally agreed that they knew little of football and would depend on business acumen to turn the franchise into a money-maker. Their first move was to fire then head coach Gus Dorais (remembered for the first forward pass in college ball to Notre Dame's Knute Rockne) and begin the search for a more talented and colorful leader, a real motivator who could turn the losing Lions into a winner. The prospects included such names as Wally Butts of Georgia, Eddie Anderson of Iowa, Paul Brown of Cleveland and Frank Leahy of Notre Dame. But finally, they were attracted to the only man who had twice coached the College All Stars to wins over the professional champs. In 1938 his collegians had drubbed the Washington Redskins and in 1946 he embarrassed the supposedly invincible Los Angeles Rams. And apart from a legendary career as player and successful college coach, his talent as an after dinner speaker proved the added consideration that brought Bo to the attention of the Lion management. Edwin Anderson, one of the syndicate members, had been moved to tears by a McMillin oration at a sales convention for beer salesmen and there decided if the man could speak so movingly to hardened businessmen, he could certainly inspire a football team to produce. Subsequently, some of the syndicate visited Bo in Bloomington to feel him out on the Lion coaching job.

The *Detroit News* noted that Bo made a "surprise visit" to Detroit's Book Cadillac Hotel to meet with Anderson for a "discussion of football" on 10 February 1948. Reputedly a tentative meeting only, with no offer being made, Bo described it as "a perfectly honorable visit," adding "that he was strictly a college man…[and declaring that] there was little likelihood that he would take a professional job at this time." He implied that he was there only to assist with his opinion of coaches being considered. His circumspect disclaimer did little to contain the rumors flying around the campus, nor did it quiet muttering over the seven years remaining on his present contract with Indiana University. His comment notwithstanding, the situation was a commentary on the futility of contracts and recalled to mind a previous criticism that this coach was no respecter of contractual obligations. One Indiana official sourly observed, "Those contracts are strange. They're one-way far as the coach is concerned but they are two-way as far as the university is concerned." Despite the grumbling that surfaced, Bo's quickening interest would bring him back to Detroit, along with some of his staff, for a second conference.

By 17 February, it was reported that McMillin was attempting to secure his release from the Indiana contract. This proved no problem, for informal polls of the Athletic Committee members and the Board of Trustees revealed no one disposed to hold him to his contract. Bo had always been acquisitive in money matters and the attraction of the big pro football salaries grew stronger than his loyalties to Indiana. Wrestling with his impending decision, he balanced what he called "the sentiment of intercollegiate football" against the security a higher salary would offer his family and concluded, "I must think of my family." His children now numbered five, after the births of Nugent in 1934 and Michael in 1942, and he felt keenly his obligation to see them through school. Still, the break with Indiana would not be easy, as he reluctantly admitted. "I'm a sentimental man, and it's hard to even think of giving all this up. In thirty-eight years in football, man and boy, this is my toughest decision." He added, in his familiar Texas vernacular, "It's corn-cob rough."

The Lions softened Bo's anguish over leaving Indiana with the offer of a five year contract at $30,000 a year. An informal agreement was quickly reached when he came to Detroit on 18 February and, on the following day, signed a contract which was conditional upon his release by Indiana University. If all went as planned, he would assume the duties of head coach on 1 March. McMillin must have notified Indiana University at once of the signing, for on the same day, F.T. Reed, assistant to the president, wired Herman Wells in Washington of Bo's action. Wells, who had been preoccupied in Germany as a cultural affairs advisor, had just recently returned to Washington and missed all of Bo's negotiations. Some grumbled that had his old friend Wells been on hand, the outcome might have been different. McMillin's letter of resignation to the Board was on its way the next day. He asked to be relieved of his athletic director duties on 1 March and those of head football coach on 1 April 1948. He ended the letter saying, "I take with me many and fond memories and you may rest assured that I will always be one of the best friends and staunchest supporters of Indiana and her athletic teams." For one so easily moved to tears of joy or sadness, these words must have caused his eyes to mist as he signed. The uncertainty over, he told one reporter, "I can tell you truthfully I have been sweating blood for 10 days now making my decision to accept the position with the Lions." On the other hand, one writer, minimizing the difficulty of the choice, quipped that the deciding factor was simply the Detroit Lions did not "have to play Minnesota, Notre Dame, and Michigan one-two-three this season." Indiana football prospects being what they were at the time, the comment made sense.

Characteristically, these dramatic negotiations did not deter McMillin from his appointed rounds. He was off on 21 February to Ames, Iowa to speak to the Iowa State College. Bo's sense of mission about football was as obvious as his love of the game. Even as he prepared to leave the pleasant college scene for the commercialism of the professional wars, the idea of the redemptive quality of football, of its moral value, of its character-molding possibilities surfaced in his comments. At one interview, ignoring the professional context with all it implied, the old idealism was plain: "I firmly believe this Detroit football job will give me the opportunity to continue doing for boys all the things I have been doing in college." And the same motif of his coaching philosophy was repeated in a later remark: "The position at Detroit offers a new challenge. These boys, although perhaps a little older, still need...guidance." As always, he viewed the job of coaching as much an ethical exercise as a physical one, and was so imbued with a sense of its didactic value that he had no qualms over his ability to continue his mission in the NFL.

The news of his leaving spread swiftly over the campus, bringing shock and the realization that an era was ending. McMillin had been a campus fixture through so many graduating classes and had accumulated so many lasting friendships among them that the thought of his departure saddened not only the student body but a host of alumni as well. The *Bloomington Star-Courier*, reflecting a sense of rejection, headlined, "Bo Abandons I.U." The article declared that Indiana had "forever lost the man who brought it more athletic recognition and prestige, more fame and fortune, more athletic headlines and history than any one individual linked with this school." But coming nearer to the sense of melancholy that crept like fog over campus and town, the report ended, saying, "It's the end of an era in Indiana football, the McMillin Age and a tradition within itself. It's little wonder that on every street corner, in every office and classroom where townspeople and students and University staff gather they have on their lips the puzzling question: 'Where will we get another one like Bo?' "

The regret was not unanimous, however. Some of the unhappy alumni who had long opposed the coach quickly made their opinions clear to the Board of Trustees. One delighted alumnus wrote the president of the Board that McMillin's leaving would permit replacing him with a "coach whose feet will be on the ground and...[whose] powers to make after dinner speeches will be a second consideration." The writer went on to describe him as a "side show attraction" who had been unable to deliver as expected, and he acidly complained that many alumni felt "too much has been sacrificed for the grandstanding and three sheeting of the famed coach."

Another alumnus remarked that a distinct service had been rendered the University in McMillin's leaving, that Indiana would now be "free to get a program under way that will create harmony and promote loyalty all around." Yet another predicted he would not last three years at Detroit, and while grudgingly admitting that he had not been "an entire failure at the University," maintained that "his mediocre showing with the wealth of material he has had indicates clearly that he is not a high class coach." As always, the coach ignored such criticism, but had he wanted to, he could have reminded this critic of the difficult war years that began Indiana's climb to the title and of the thirty-man squads of freshmen and 4-F's who did it.

Even the president of the Board of Trustees, concurring with a critical alumnus' letter, replied, "I share your view that no one is indispensable." Quite clearly, future events belied his opinion, for neither he nor the complaining alumni could have foreseen the precipitous decline in Indiana football that followed Bo's departure. It would be a long ten years before IU could savor a winning season again.

Reporters from the *Indiana Daily Student* wandered the campus interviewing many for their thoughts on the coach's leaving. The cross section of opinion revealed that he had had both staunch adherents and confirmed critics, that there was no middle ground. The dean of students said, "It will be difficult to think of football at IU without this colorful coach. His high ideals and moral standards have been a fine example to our student body." The secretary of the Alumni Association gave the laconic response, "I guess it's too bad, but I guess that there is somebody just as good around the corner." But the dean of the School of Health summarized the opinion of most: "I think that we are losing one of the finest football coaches in the United States."

This last comment more nearly captured the student attitude, for the general feeling on campus was one of numb loss. No more would Hoosier fans laugh at and cheer Bo's bobbing antics on the bench: yelling encouragement to his players, striding the sideline in nervous worry, weeping unashamed tears of joy in victory, or brushing off defeat. No more would his warm Texas drawl enchant and promise better things. No more would they marvel at his football cunning, his ability to inspire his teams to more than their best. Most agreed and long remembered that Bo had brought football greatness to Indiana and that his record was the shrine of his years there.

McMillin returned to campus on 23 February to a pile of telegrams and scores of phone calls from well-wishers. He took time to attend a special meeting with Indiana's varsity lettermen, urging them to continue to play with the same spirit and determination that they had shown in the past. Then he returned to a theme so familiar to those young men: "The important thing is that you get your education, and prepare yourselves the best you know how for what is to follow." The charge was an echo of his statement in an earlier interview that day. Though the syntax limped, the sincerity of the message was clear: "I have always tried to do for young boys what another once did for me, encourage boys to live up to their fullest capacities. There is no greater job for any man than in watching these young men move into the world that follows college athletic competition and make a success of their endeavor."

Nothing approaching the giant reception that had welcomed him marked the exit of Indiana's most successful football coach. Only several small appreciation dinners sponsored by Sigma Chi and his own fraternity, Beta Theta Pi, noted McMillin's departure. He returned in March to speak to the annual IU football and basketball teams' appreciation banquet that the Downtown Coaches Club sponsored. If there was any swan song, this must have been it. And thus an era of Indiana football passed quietly into history. Leaving by breaking his contractual obligation clashed with Bo's reputed rectitude and unsettled many of his admirers, but not even this could blemish the memories this feisty football genius left behind.

The wire the new coach of the Lions received from Jimmy Conzelman, coach of the pro champion Chicago Cardinals, set the tone of the next chapter in his career: "Welcome to the rat race."

CHAPTER NINE

In the Lions' Den

(1948-1950)

*Football was the warp and woof of McMillin's existence,
and while such absorption might seem trifling to some, to
the little Praying Colonel it was Napoleon before Water-
loo, Lee at Chancellorsville, and Petain declaring they
would not pass at Verdun.*

Hugh Brown

When Bo McMillin signed his contract with the Detroit Lions, his experience had convinced him that there existed little difference between collegiate and professional football. Indeed, he saw
them growing closer together as the colleges played in larger and
larger stadiums and increasingly found new ways to subsidize players.
He was soon to discover how mistaken he had been. However much
commercialized, the college game, nurtured in an environment of
youthful enthusiasm and school spirit, and supported by an annually
augmented alumni, still thrived on emotion and dedication. By contrast, the National Football League struggled for survival in the harsh
world of business enterprise where uneasy team owners hired and
fired coaches, dropped and traded players, or bought and sold franchises in a quest for profit and sometimes personal gratification. If
McMillin was to succeed in Detroit, he must motivate men who played
for money rather than for alma mater, fill the stands with paying cus-
tomers, and please a Board of Directors, who, balance sheet in hand,
would always be looking over his shoulder. And he must accomplish
all of this under the eyes of a press that would hold up his past success
as a measure of his current accomplishments.

He went to the Lions during a major transition in the National Football League. Founded in 1920, the League had by 1939 overcome its shaky beginning, the battering of the Great Depression, and the challenge of rival leagues to achieve stability with an average attendance of 20,000 a game. A wide-open game with more spectator appeal had come with the introduction of the T-formation and with several departures from the college rules in order to make the forward pass the major offensive weapon. Dividing the League into two divisions with a playoff for the championship had increased regional interest, as did the network radio broadcasts of some games in 1940. And to strike better team balance, a system of drafting college players promised a more even distribution of player talent. The shortage of manpower during World War II was answered by permitting unlimited substitution, an innovation that soon introduced player specialists. At the end of the War attendance swelled to nearly double the 1939 average, and the move of the Cleveland Rams to Los Angeles in 1946 spread the NFL from coast to coast. Also that year, the Rams broke the color barrier by signing two black players, a change that over the next few seasons would greatly enlarge the pool of player talent. Yet, when Bo McMillin took over the Lions in 1948, the NFL's prosperity was threatened by a fierce bidding war for players with a new rival, the American Football Conference.

Some who knew McMillin's methods well doubted that he could easily make the transfer from college coaching to the NFL. Among them, Heartley W. (Hunk) Anderson, who had played for the Chicago Bears and coached at Notre Dame, warned that Bo will "soon discover that this is an entirely different racket than coaching college football. He'll have to learn all over and it will take time." Such warnings only increased McMillin's determination to prove them wrong. He reached Detroit on 26 February and set to work. Too busy to find a home and move his family at first, he lived for several months with close friend Elden Auker, his Kansas State player and a former pitcher for the Detroit Tigers.

Once again McMillin would attempt to turn around a losing team. The year following the club's 1934 move from Portsmouth, Ohio, to Detroit, the Lions had won the NFL championship, but the team had never enjoyed such success again. The last two years, under coach Gus Dorais, the Notre Dame immortal, the Lions had suffered through 1-10 and 3-9 seasons. Outwardly unworried at the prospect of starting over, McMillin told reporters, "I've taken over down-at-the-heel clubs all my life — Centenary, Geneva, Kansas State, and yes — even Indiana." His characteristic openness and sincerity in his initial news conference prompted one photographer to comment, "Seems a shame to toss a quiet little fellow like that into this dog-eat-dog professional football league, doesn't it?"

A quarter century afterwards, President Edwin Anderson, for some unknown reason, insisted that McMillin had never been made general manager of the Lions in addition to his coaching duties. Yet the Lion stationery was headed "A. N. McMillin, Gen. Mgr.," and the press at the time had no doubt about his status. In the past, the ticket manager had also been acting as general manager, so some confusion over the exact title may have developed later. In any case, McMillin clearly assumed full control over the operations of the club.

He first announced that he would replace the entire coaching staff with his own. One assistant, veteran line coach Joseph Bach, had been five years with the Lions and previously the head coach of the Pittsburgh Steelers. Some thought that Bo was losing a wealth of professional experience by releasing Bach, but he was determined to start fresh with his own crew. He named his two assistants from Indiana to the new staff, Owen L. (Chili) Cochrane, backfield coach, and C. A. (Timmy) Temerario, line coach, explaining, "If I am to be successful, it is necessary for me to gather around me, as members of my staff, men with whom I have had long acquaintance and who know my strong and weak points." Equipment manager Roy Macklem, a holdover and never an admirer, later stressed as one of McMillin's weak points his never asking for suggestions or advice from his coaches. He ran the show so much that Macklem wondered why he had assistant coaches at all. The criticism was accurate, for in college McMillin had dominated his coaching staff with his attention to detail. It would be no different in the NFL.

After being fired, Dorais had written a series of articles for *The Detroit News* analyzing the Lions' problems, pointing mainly to the lack of players of the quality needed to win. The new coach was well aware of the shortage of first rate talent and launched a search. College recruiting had always been a McMillin specialty. His talent for after dinner speaking was widely recognized and always created something of a forum for his remarkable "ability to snare the...super-duper sons of

other men to play on his college football teams." While the strong con-
tacts of the rookie pro coach in collegiate circles would help, obviously, recruiting in the NFL was vastly different. Here the success of
the player draft each winter and the competitive enticement of salary
loomed larger than Bo's emotional appeals. Also, the normal off-season business of player trading in the league became a mine field with
the presence of tough, old professional veterans like Steve Owen of the
New York Giants, George Halas of the Chicago Bears, Jimmy Conzelman of the Chicago Cardinals, Greasy Neale of the Philadelphia
Eagles, and Curly Lambeau of the Green Bay Packers. It would take
some serious sleight-of-hand to get the better of a trade in such company. McMillin's way was not smoothed, either, by the fact that twice
his College All-Stars had humbled the National Football League
champions, nor that he had irritated its coaches by freely asserting the
superiority of college players over professionals.

Nonetheless, McMillin did enjoy some recruiting success in his
first year. In July he traded regulars Frank Szymanski, a center from
Notre Dame, and Ted Cook, an end from Alabama, to Green Bay for
Howard Brown, an excellent guard, and Bob Rennebaum, an end from
Wisconsin. The key to this exchange was Brown, who had played four
seasons for Bo at Indiana and was a devoted admirer of the man and his
methods. He also picked up All-American end Bob Mann from Michigan, and guard Les Bingaman of Illinois. Of the early additions,
Bingaman became a testimony to Bo's eye for talent when he later became one of the most respected linemen in the league. In the spring
draft he selected Y.A. Tittle, from Louisiana State, as a solution to the
Lions' previous year's difficulty at quarterback. But the future all-time
star refused the lackluster Lions out of hand to sign with the Baltimore
Colts of the rival All-America Conference. McMillin's talent search
led him to seek another player destined for greatness, quarterback
Bobby Layne, who was currently setting records with the University
of Texas. Bo had watched him in the All-Star Game and commented,
"Gee, I wish we had him. You just watch that boy go in this league!"
But Layne was drafted by the Pittsburgh Steelers and, refusing to go
there, was subsequently traded to Halas's Chicago Bears. A surplus
rookie quarterback there, he languished on the bench behind two great
ones, Sid Luckman and Johnny Lujack. Beginning a pursuit that
would continue for several seasons, in August Bo offered the Bears

what he described as "an awful lot of money" for Layne, but the overture was spurned by Halas. However, in those money-tight days a $15,000 bench-warmer was a luxury no professional team could afford, so late in the season the Bears peddled Layne to the floundering New York Bulldogs, who were without a quarterback. Though Layne moved around, he was never out of sight or plan of McMillin. But for the 1948 season, Bo would have to make do with what he had.

On 1 August McMillin took a squad of nearly sixty players, almost half rookies, to the campus of Alma College in north central Michigan to begin preparing for his first professional season. He brought to this camp the same intensity with which he had prepared college teams. Veterans were at once put on notice that their places were not secure. Training camp was short and quickly followed by a brief exhibition season during which the Lions showed some promise. They dominated the Steelers 38-10, lost a "squeaker" to the Philadelphia Eagles 35-37, and whipped the New York Giants 28-20. In assessing the result, McMillin candidly admitted that the defense was ahead of his offense, a problem he would work on. But, as is usually the case, the exhibition season was no real test; it was a shakedown for the rookies, a tryout of new formations, a time of looking and evaluating. The actual time of testing lay ahead.

The regular season opened in Los Angeles on 22 September against the Rams, and the debut turned into a rout as the Lions fumbled six times and lost 44-7. This was the worst defeat Bo McMillin had ever suffered as a player or coach. It ended all of his illusions about the parity of college and professional football. The season continued in a disheartening series of lopsided losses, as McMillin, frustrated by his weakness at quarterback and hampered by a growing list of players sidelined by injuries, fought a losing battle.

The Lions won their first game in a year on the last Sunday of October after an exhausting struggle with the Green Bay Packers, the thirtieth time these traditional antagonists had met. But McMillin found little enjoyment in his initial win as a professional coach. The team had already lost three players to broken bone injuries and this game added three more. The next week the Chicago Cardinals administered an unmerciful beating to the crippled Lions, 56-20.

Against the Cardinals, the Lions had worn new red and black uniforms. The equipment manager, Macklem, years later was harshly critical of the change from the Lions' traditional blue and grey to Indiana's red and black. Furthermore, he remembered that McMillin had purchased the cheapest material available, and, as a result, the jerseys fell apart before the season was half over. He further recalled that the coach searched for and found $8.00 headgear (when good ones cost $15.00), ones so cheap "even high schools would have laughed at them." Macklem insisted that such parsimony resulted from a profit-sharing deal the coach and general manager had with the owners, an account one of them denied totally. McMillin was famous among his friends for his frugality, but it is difficult to believe that he would have jeopardized the safety of his players.

The following week the Washington Redskins, led by Sammy Baugh, trampled the hapless Lions 46-21. To McMillin any loss was bad enough, but these lopsided scores were devastating. On 21 November, at Briggs Stadium, the Lions finally snapped back with a win over the Steelers 17-14; not too impressive, but a win, at least. The dismal season had won Detroit few fans, and only 16,189 had seen this game. Then on Thanksgiving Day, the Chicago Cards crushed McMillin's team again, 28-14, before 22,967. Although public interest in professional football was growing, the Lions still could not compete with the nearby University of Michigan Wolverines in either attendance or press coverage. Even a high school game in Detroit on Thanksgiving Day outdrew the Lions-Cards game. Detroit ended the season by losing to the Philadelphia Eagles 45-21 and finished last in the league with two wins and ten losses.

Not all the sports writers were as fair-minded as H.G. Salsinger in the *Detroit News* who, reviewing the season, wrote, "Considering the limited material that Alvin (Bo) McMillin had at his command, the fact that the Lions won any game is highly commendable....No coach is better than his material." No one was more aware of that truth than the Lions' coach. He made an early move to get the draft rights to Doak Walker, Southern Methodist University's great back. Since Walker still had another year of college eligibility and would not be available until then, the *Detroit News* took Bo to task, expressing "wonderment" at his trading current high draft choices for a long term gamble. But McMillin was planning ahead. In addition to Walker, he drafted twenty-three other players at the league meeting in Philadelphia. By the end of 1948, he had put the disastrous season behind him and was directing his energies toward the rebuilding that this fresh talent made possible.

One of the perquisites Bo enjoyed with his job was membership in the posh Bloomfield Hills Country Club. Although he thoroughly enjoyed its fine golf course and played acceptably there, the annual meeting of the membership gave him an opportunity to demonstrate another skill for which he was noted. Once the business of the meeting concluded, a large group of members customarily retired to the locker room for a serious dice game. Edwin Anderson recalled that these locker room games would go on until four or five in the morning with McMillin in the thick of it the whole time, winning more often than not. Suite 634 at the Detroit Athletic Club was also home to frequent crap shooting and card playing by the Lion management. There the coach gave the owners many expensive lessons in the art of craps. He had almost cut his teeth on dice and was known from boyhood as an expert. Gambling was serious business to Bo, and if his preoccupation with football permitted any hobby, it had to be gambling. Gambling was not a moral issue with him; he enjoyed it as simply another sport and demonstrated the same competitiveness with dice that marked his football.

Undoubtedly, critics of Bo would recognize in his love of gambling and his spotless sportsmanship a serious personal dichotomy. And the gambling made a poor companion for his devout Catholic faith and practice as well. But if his gambling is looked on as an extension of his innate desire to win, at whatever game, it seems less at odds with his standard of athletic morality.

For the sport fan a football season begins and ends in the fall, but for the NFL coach it is year-round with no respite from the constant pressure of planning and talent hunting. The first week of 1949 found Bo at the Cotton Bowl, pursuing Doak Walker and again failing to get a commitment from him to join the Lions upon graduation. By the end of January Bo reported that his talent hunt was ending with fifteen newly-signed players. The new season's team would begin to reflect his imprint, for his selections now represented two-thirds of the squad. February found him spending his three week "vacation" roaming the Texas campuses during spring football practice, prospecting for future draft choices, an ongoing chore no professional coach could ignore. It may have been less than a chore for Bo, for he was working familiar ground; the Lone Star State was home.

In the spring of 1949, McMillin made two moves that strengthened the Lion organization. First, he created a farm system in an affiliate agreement with the Wilkes-Barre, Pennsylvania team of the American Football League. The NFL player limit had recently been cut from thirty-five to thirty-two, and the affiliation gave Bo a place to hold additional borderline players for further training and prompt recall. Considering the past season's record of disabling injuries, the association was good insurance. Then in May McMillin signed George Wilson (who would some years later become head coach of the Lions) as an assistant coach, replacing Lou Zarza. Bo took Wilson away from George Halas after he had served twelve years as an end coach with the Bears. Also, by now nineteen recruits had been signed to fill out the roster.

Sixty players assembled at training camp at the end of July, a surprising thirty-nine of them rookies. One of these, Cloyce Box, a rookie halfback from West Texas State, came to Bo in an unusual trade that would prove memorable. Having no spot for Box, George Preston Marshall offered him to a suspicious McMillin for an unbelievably low figure. Wary of being out-traded by the wily chief of the Washington Redskins, Bo countered with half the amount and, perhaps to his surprise, purchased for pocket money a player who would go on to become one of the Lions' greatest pass receivers of all time.

Training camp was an abbreviated affair. In a short seventeen days, the Lions would have to be ready for their first exhibition game. After the usual conditioning, on the third day Bo surprised the players with a tough scrimmage. He meant business. They either had to share his dedication or suffer its consequences. Columnist H. G. Salsinger, after watching the camp, questioned the quality of the players assembled. But McMillin was quietly confident as he responded, "We expect to improve upon last year's record. We should be better this season." Another sportswriter, Watson Spoelstra, after seeing the group, minced no words, calling them the "down-at-the-heels Lions, who need help desperately."

So it seemed when the club was embarrassed in its first two exhibition games. The second of these, on Saturday, September 3 with the Philadelphia Eagles in New Orleans, presented Bo with an unfamiliar problem. He had two fine black players, end Bob Mann, and halfback Mel Groomes, both excellent athletes, but New Orleans had never witnessed an integrated game. McMillin had been advised that the decision was his to play them or not. According to Bob Mann, he called both of them to his office, obviously worried by the decision that was his. Reluctantly, he told them not to suit up, that he wasn't going to be a pioneer. Mann felt that Bo had a chance "to make a 'statement' and didn't," that the avoidance seemed out of character. But a gracious Bob Mann years later confided that he would have been offended by Bo's decision except for "the kind of man Bo was." He knew it was society's fault, not Bo's.

Only a win over the Giants in the final exhibition contest gave Bo cause to hope that his rebuilding efforts might be successful. The continuing weakness at quarterback still undercut the finest coaching he could give. A worried McMillin watched his Lions lose four straight as the regular season progressed. But despite the poor record, the careful observer began to find signs that a cohesive football team was emerging. Even the usually critical *Detroit News* reported that performance so far seemed to "confirm Bo McMillin's summertime boast that we'll have an improved ball club."

That opinion was vindicated the following week when the Lions trounced the Chicago Cards 24-7. One newspaper marked the event with the headline, "Lions do it at last!" It was their first league win since 21 November 1948 — a long dry spell — and Bo had been thirsty the whole time. Unfortunately, it was a win streak of one, for the Packers narrowly topped the Lions the next weekend 16-14. This up and down performance caused H. G. Salsinger to attempt an explanation: "To date the Detroit Lions have been an unlucky team. Mechanically and temperamentally they are better than last year, but the breaks have been against them." McMillin had to be pleased that someone else had noticed, for the close games, the bad breaks, the injuries, all had clouded the progress being made. But the persistent quarterback problem grew more critical as Bo watched the Lions battle and lose to some of the league's finest in that position — Sid Luckman, Y.A. Tittle, and Bobby Layne.

The season wearied on in a one-sided loss to Buddy Parker's Chicago Cards that the newspapers called the "worst game of the year," and continued with further losses to the Chicago Bears and the New

York Bulldogs. Then, just when McMillin began wondering if he would ever bring home a win, his team surprised everyone by beating the tough Green Bay Packers, 21-7, in the season finale. The win meant the Lions finished out of the cellar for the first time in four years with a 4-8 record. Although not one to cheer about, it was evidence that a corner had been turned.

What progress had been made must be credited to Bo's constant efforts to upgrade personnel. At season's end the team included twenty-four players of his selection with only twelve carry-overs from the Dorais period. He was gradually surrounding himself with personnel that suited his type of play. He knew there were no overnight cures and had warned that remaking the Lions would take time. The 1949 season had won him no laurels, but he was beginning to see progress.

The year ended with the merger of the National Football League and the All-America Conference. It was less merger than absorption, for the AAC had been struggling against impossible odds, and finally, in financial disaster, quit. Only three AAC franchises, Cleveland, San Francisco, and Baltimore, came into the new organization, now renamed the National American Football League. The Lion coach had visions of grabbing a quarterback out of the AAC collapse, but nothing materialized, and he remained in trouble at this position.

No assignment of the new year was more important to McMillin than his attendance at the first convention of NAFL delegates. It was crucial that he prevent the league shakeup from affecting his existing draft rights to big Leon Hart, the great end from Notre Dame, and Southern Methodist's star back, Doak Walker. At the same time, he was trying to get the rights to Vince Banonis, the All-American center from the University of Detroit. By 21 January Hart was reported ready to sign with the Lions, and the following day, to McMillin's relief, the Lions' draft right to Walker was confirmed. But the matter still dragged on unresolved, for, though drafted, he had not yet committed himself. In the midst of these negotiations, Bo pulled off a trade that upset many Detroiters and brought him a bundle of criticism from the press. He swapped one of his established running backs, Bill Dudley, for Dan Sandifer of the Redskins. Brushing the criticism aside, Mc-Millin simply pointed out that Sandifer was younger and faster, qualities important to his type of play. In another move that raised some questions, he traded to the Philadelphia Eagles his number one draft choice for Lindell Pearson, a back from Oklahoma. It was a gamble, but that was football. Also while at the Philadelphia draft meeting, he employed recently-fired Buddy Parker as an assistant backfield coach, a move that would soon be McMillin's undoing with the Detroit club.

At a meeting with the local press following the draft, Lion executive Edwin Anderson revealed that his club had lost $200,000 in the last two years and stated flatly that unless there was better public support, "we are through." It was less threat than simple statement of fact. His businessmen partners in the syndicate expected profits, not deficits and, if necessary, were prepared to cut their losses. Despite his pessimistic talk to the reporters, Anderson indicated that the Lions were continuing to chase after Bobby Layne. But this pursuit was only one aspect of McMillin's recruiting efforts. His continuing work on Walker, while coaching the Senior Bowl in Jacksonville, finally paid off, for on 26 February it was announced that Ewell Doak Walker had signed with the Lions for $12,000. Added to this good news was the signing of sought-after Leon Hart on a similar three year contract. McMillin's stock as a pro recruiter rose with these two impressive additions to the Lions' roster.

In the midst of his off-season preoccupation with draft, recruiting, and tactical planning, McMillin still found time to hit the banquet trail occasionally, sometimes with amusing consequences. Once in February 1950 in Toledo, a worried McMillin phoned the *Toledo Times* asking, "Say, where am I supposed to speak tonight?" A quick check of the hotels and clubs revealed no McMillin date. Puzzled, he persisted, "I came here to talk to some meeting — try again." Still nothing. Finally, McMillin wondered, "Maybe I have the wrong date." A further check proved him right; he was two weeks early for a talk with the Toledo Foremen's Club. As the *Indianapolis News* captioned the story, "Right church, wrong pew."

In July, Lion prospects continued to brighten as McMillin's old Indiana star, Bob Hoernschemeyer, verbally agreed to sign. He made a fine addition to the offense and was destined to become another one of Detroit's future greats. The talented core of the Lion championship teams of the early Fifties was gradually coming together. Bo knew he was getting close.

McMillin's recruiting successes were capped that season when his long pursuit of Bobby Layne finally ended. Chairing a meeting of the board of directors, McMillin surprised them by announcing that he had a chance to buy Layne from the New York Bulldogs for $37,500, the amount still due Halas's Chicago Bears on the original purchase price. Despite their lack of a talented quarterback, the shaky financial condition of the Lions found the directors vehemently opposed. The team already had three quarterbacks, their objections ran: Freddie Enge and two backups.

The discussion reached fever pitch as McMillin sat listening in silence. Finally, without a word, he reached into his coat pocket and pulled out his contract and pointedly smoothed it beside his coffee cup. An observer called it "the most dramatic thing....[he'd] ever seen business-wise." In the sudden silence that ensued, there could be no mistaking Bo's meaning; the directors knew that the contract guaranteed him absolute autonomy in player selection, and they knew exactly what was at stake. After a few seconds pause, McMillin said the chair would entertain a motion that Detroit purchase Bobby Layne for $37,500, payable to George Halas. There was silence, then a nervous cough or two, a throat clearing, and finally, a "so move." After another pregnant pause, a "second" followed. Looking around the table, McMillin inquired, "Now is there any discussion?" Again silence, for the previous heated discussion had emptied the objections. Then on the question, the directors unanimously approved. Still without ever referring to it, McMillin picked up the contract and put it back in his pocket. While McMillin's show of power in quashing opposition to the Layne acquisition won the day, it is quite possible that he sowed the seeds of resentment among the the directors that later would do him in.

Finally, after so long, Layne belonged to the Lions, and McMillin was sure now that the future belonged to him. Yet in the midst of all the upbeat news, there remained the nagging observation by some that as far as Bo was concerned, it was "no secret that the head coach of the Lions....[was] on the spot of the year." After two unsuccessful seasons he had to produce. But at least now McMillin faced the coming league season with a team of possibility.

When training camp began that fall *Detroit News* sportswriter H. G. Salsinger looked over the player roster and observed, "It is not the largest squad but the best that the Lions have ever assembled for training." This time it was a McMillin squad; of the fifty-seven players on hand, only five were from 1948 and ten from 1949. Clearly, the 1950 season would be the first real test of his recruiting and coaching. A Lions news release reflected the general view: "This [the large number of new faces] provides concrete evidence that Bo McMillin has done a pretty thorough job of house-cleaning to secure what he believes to be his type of football player." Whether they were his type was less apparent to the Detroit football fan than the obvious fact that the Lions now had a roster that included some top talent: Leon Hart of Notre Dame, Doak Walker of Southern Methodist, Aldo Forte of Montana, Joe Watson of Rice, Lou Creekmur of William & Mary, Bobby Hoernschemeyer of Indiana, Thurman McGraw of Colorado A&M, Cloyce Box of West Texas State, and Les Bingaman of Illinois. And now with the linchpin of the rebuilding effort, Bobby Layne at quarterback, McMillin felt that he had his team.

The start of the 1950 exhibition season again disappointed as the Lions fell first to the Redskins and then to the Eagles, despite the presence of Layne. The final game with the Chicago Cards restored some confidence as Layne's passing brought home a win, 24-16, but even an optimist like McMillin could scarcely call the exhibition season a success.

While the regular season had some high spots, it suffered some low ones, such as the October loss to the Rams 65-24, the highest points posted against the Lions in seventeen years and the third highest in the history of the league. The forty-one points scored by the Rams in the third quarter is still the league record for a quarter. More serious than the aches and pains acquired were the egos bruised. McMillin did not have records like this in mind when he took on the job. Small wonder that within the week rumors began to fly that their coach would be fired unless the Lions beat the Bears next week. The stories of impending dismissal worried Bo less than the problem of readying a badly beaten team for the game; the Bears were tough and on a winning streak. Rumors of McMillin's demise mushroomed after 5 November when the Bears humbled the Lions 35-21 before 30,000 imploring fans.

Characteristically, despite the loss, the Lion coach was still the optimist. He maintained that there was still a year or two of rebuilding to do. His players, he said, had been beaten by experience, but his confident words conflicted with a *News* post-game photo capturing the strain on his face.

The season finale on 10 December again pitted the Lions against the high-riding Bears, a contest carrying significance far beyond that of a single game. For the Bears (who had won nine straight) a victory could force a playoff for divisional honors, while for the Lions, a win meant posting a 7-5 season (the best in five years), earning some needed respectability, and giving substance to the growing belief that their 1951 team would have championship possibilities. And finally, for Bo personally, a win would quiet the persistent rumors that his days were numbered. It was a high stakes game, grimly fought, which saw the Lions hold the Bears to a single touchdown. Although a moral victory of sorts for the Lions, the Bears won on the scoreboard, 6-3. The gloom of the Lion dressing room was not improved by the absence after the game of Edwin Anderson, who normally visited the players in victory or defeat. Somehow it seemed that more had been lost than just the final game. In public and private, game post-mortems concluded with scrutiny of Bo's work with the Lions.

Throughout these three seasons McMillin had brought a new kind of coaching to professional football that went beyond an adjustment to his well-known "cockeyed T." Just as he had in his college coaching days, he sought playing excellence on the field and expected a high standard of personal conduct from his players off the field as well. But the professional athlete was older, wiser, and, freed of the constraints of the college environment, less inclined to go along with the rules his coach imposed. Aware of the number of youngsters who gathered outside the Lions' dressing room, McMillin forbade cigaret smoking by players as they left their quarters. He was just as opposed to their drinking in public bars and night clubs. "You're the finest young athletes in the city and you must act that way," he would tell them. "I don't want to see any Lion walking out of the stadium with a cigaret hanging from his lip. I don't want you to even smoke or drink, but if you do, you must not make a public show of uninspiring practices."

It was a personal standard that many of the players did not share. In particular, Texan Bobby Layne was a free spirit, unwilling to heel to such a code. While he admitted Bo was "a great college coach," he felt that this strictness was the root of his lack of rapport in coaching the Lions. Layne complained that McMillin handled professional players "just as he would a college team and would never change." He pointed to three hour practices in the cold, and said that "might be all right in college with a ten game schedule, but...[it was] pretty difficult when you play 20 or 22 games in pro ball." Layne became the renegade who each Monday afternoon assembled most of the Lions for "revelry and camaraderie" at the Stadium Bar. Layne claimed even non-drinkers like Doak Walker showed up for the fun. Other patrons were excused from these sessions which sometimes drifted noisily to another location as festivities warmed. It is probable that from these get-togethers sprang Layne's ultimate playing field leadership of the Lions. It is also likely that these assemblies were the birthplace of the player "revolt" to come.

Layne's pre-game carousing became common knowledge and must have been difficult for Bo to accept. It certainly had no place in the coach's personal code of careful preparation, physical fitness, and mental dedication. In Layne he was forced to accommodate an exceptional athlete who broke all the rules, yet went out on Sunday and performed with brilliance. It was the consummate incongruity that a straight arrow like McMillin should be harnessed to an iconoclast like Layne. The resulting friction of personalities was not one to be overcome; it simply had to be endured, and Bo knew it.

Inevitably, it became obvious that, in the professional environment, the old player-coach, father-son relationship was no longer relevant. The realization must have hurt, for it was on this emotional base that McMillin had built teams that could be inspired to reach for excellence beyond their talents. To a large extent, this natural bent for squeezing exceptional performance from his players was compromised, and, certainly, some of the exhilaration he found in the game was gone. He was not unaware of his difficulty in relating to his players. Later, upon his resignation from the Lions, his statement acknowledged the fact: "It has been said and printed that some of my players did not like or respect me....While coaching the Lions I was not conducting a popularity contest....I had to say no. I had to mete out the discipline. Therefore I am not surprised that some gossip-mongers would pick up rumors from a few malcontents that I was unpopular."

The rumors had more than a little foundation in fact. Once while on a trip to the west coast, McMillin's team meeting was interrupted by a visit from the club president and assistant coach George Wilson, who were a bit in their cups. When the visitors insisted the team sing the Lion fight song, it was obvious that most of the players knew their playbook better than the fight song. Bo's reaction won no supporters, for he imposed a $25 fine on anyone who did not know the words the next time asked. Surprisingly, the teetotalling coach took less offense at the drunken interruption than to his "boys" not knowing the "school" song. Perhaps the judgment of one observer was right, that he "tried to make a college team out of them."

Bo had other signs indicating that rapport with his players, so cherished by him, just was not there. At the season's end in 1949, the players had presented Lou Cromwell, who handled equipment and trip arrangements, an appreciation gift of a fine hand-tooled leather valise. Bo was reportedly "flabbergasted" that they'd do that for the equipment manager and not for him. There is no way to quantify McMillin's problem with certainty, but available evidence would indicate that it could not be as easily minimized as McMillin suggested.

McMillin's method had other critics. The equipment manager, Macklem, was sharply critical of his habit of making emotional, highly charged talks to inspire the team in the half, and of his imploring the Almighty to have mercy on his team. Macklem claimed the players saw through the shallowness of it, that the tear jerking just did not work with professional athletes as it had with college teams. Macklem misunderstood; it was not an act. It was simply Bo's way. Dedication, fervor, prayer were not shallow displays. They were integral evidences of the simple honesty of the inner man. McMillin's strongly-held Catholic faith guided his life. He saw nothing incongruous in praying with his players before a game. Seeking the blessing of Divine Providence came as naturally to him in football as it did in life. When he moved to the National Football League, he carried this value system with him and preached it with the same vigor. But here the chemistry was wrong; professional football was a business, not a rite of passage. McMillin could be the coach, but not a moral leader. He still called them his "boys," but the bonding relationship was not there. Although it is possible that he sensed the change, he had spent too many years on the college scene to shift his method.

McMillin's obdurate moralism in the permissive world of pro sports alienated not only players but at times cost him support with some of the owners. On one occasion, while on a road trip to San Francisco, Bo and his wife were invited to have breakfast with one of the Lion directors, who was travelling with his girl friend rather than his wife.

Bo's reaction was in character, but scarcely tactful as he refused, saying, "My Kathryn isn't going to sit down at the same table with that woman!" While such a principled response can be understood coming from a man like McMillin, at the same time it demonstrates a lack of understanding of the reality of his position. He took cognizance of the friction with the board of directors when he told newsmen upon his leaving the Lions, "It is difficult to do your best work when members of your own official family are sniping at you."

Although it is true that the fiesty little coach had similar troubles with alumni and trustees at Indiana, almost an occupational hazard of collegiate coaching, he should have recognized that the professional relationship was different, a business one that survived in an environment of compromise and conciliation. Here the love of winning was distractingly complicated by the commercial overtones of contracts, money, gate attendance, and dollar-powered recruiting. Gone was the college esprit, the community-shared glory of winning; gone the emotional pep rallies, and the traditional rivalries of transcendent importance. Gone were the fading echoes of the "alma mater" that made eyes mist in recollection. And gone was that sheltered feeling of twilight walks amid halls of ivy. It just was not the same. Though he never said so, despite his salary, Bo must have looked back at his halcyon Indiana days with some longing.

As the 1950 season closed, in spite of the Lions' demonstrated progress, the wolves were beginning to howl. Postmortems of the season emphasized that Doak Walker had set the league record for most points scored in a rookie season, and Cloyce Box had set new pass reception records. Amazingly, this assemblage of Lions had broken forty-two of its own standing records as a team. But these impressive statistics did not quiet the rumors about Bo's future. One *Detroit News* writer did a "pro and con" column that offered an analysis of the team and its coaches. On the "pro" side, he noted a steadily improving playing record (the season had wound up a much better 6 and 6, the best record since 1945), pointed out that the club had finally made money, and admitted the strong possibility that a championship season loomed. On the noticeably shorter "con" side, he vaguely complained that the coaching staff should have gotten "better mileage" out of the squad, and pointed to the tendency to lose the close games. On balance, such an assessment did not seem too unfavorable, but the public rumblings went on. The *News* did a man-in-the-street poll; of thirty interviewed, twenty-seven favored retaining Bo. He was not without adherents.

But inevitably, after the final game of the season, the owners called a meeting at the Detroit Athletic Club to discuss the coach's future. As McMillin emerged from the meeting, he responded to reporters with a firm, "No," when asked whether he had been fired. They pressed further, "Was anybody fired?" Back came the same reply, "No." The Lions ownership met again on 18 December, Bo's future once more the subject. At meeting's end they were quoted: "McMillin's qualities as a luncheon, dinner, and banquet speaker and his general affability in meeting people are factors long appreciated by the directors." However, omitting any mention of his coaching ability made the comment less than an endorsement.

Concurrent with the ominous sounds coming from the owners' meetings was the report in the newspapers and the rumors on the street that a player "revolt" threatened. Edwin Anderson always maintained that he never was aware of it. Yet Bobby Layne was reported to have told reporters in Dallas, Texas, that he had "informed the Detroit club's directors [he] would not play under McMillin next season." He was openly critical of training methods and the handling of personnel. Layne later denied this story, but did admit that he had told the directors his team could win a championship under Parker. Big Leon Hart, when questioned years later, indicated he knew of the players' objection, but was not a part of it. He added that it was supposed to have been secret. One article of the time reported that Layne, Box, and Walker (who denied it) were part of the "original six" who joined to lay down an ultimatum in which they refused to play for McMillin. The threat caused some directors to panic, while others bristled angrily and talked of refusing to let "the men in the shop" dictate terms. In any event, the evidence strongly suggests that the players' objection weighed heavily in the directors' decision to fire their coach.

It fell to Anderson to notify McMillin. At 6 p.m. on Tuesday, 19 December 1950 the two men met at the Detroit Athletic Club. Anderson long remembered that it took until midnight to convince McMillin that he really was through. Unaccustomed to losing, he fought to stay but finally realized that he had no recourse but resignation. The Lions agreed to pay out his contract of $30,000 annually for the final two years. Suddenly Bo was unemployed; well paid, but unemployed. As expected, Buddy Parker was named the new Lion head coach. The *Detroit News* reported his salary to be $12,000 per year, so far under Bo's that it seemed to confirm, despite some denials, that McMillin had originally been hired as general manager as well as head coach.

Some post-firing stories circulated that Parker had been less than cooperative in his work with McMillin. There may have been substance to the rumors. In one incident, Nick Kerbawy (then Lion business manager), recounted McMillin's unusual request to have him attend practice and observe. After observing practice for a while, Bo asked Kerbawy if he had noticed anything unusual. Nick replied that he thought Parker just wandered off when the team came together, that he did not stick with the backfield people. McMillin agreed, "That's it; we don't seem to relate." Obviously, the relationship bothered Bo. Some close to the situation even suspected that Parker may have abetted the players' discord. One story surfaced that early in the season Bo had ordered Parker to go to Philadelphia to scout the Steelers, but, without explanation, Parker did not go. Asked why at that point he was not fired, McMillin replied that it "was early in the season, we were just getting started....I didn't want to start a ruckus, and besides, Parker is a very good backfield coach." Bo's reluctance to demand the discipline of his coach that he expected of his players may have been a major mistake.

The day after the meeting with Anderson, McMillin faced reporters and photographers. Seated at his familiar office desk piled high with Christmas cards, he released a six hundred word statement. One reporter wrote, "Nothing in his manner and little in his speech betrayed the dejection and resentment...[Bo] must have felt." A bit of irritation did surface later in the interview when, in commenting on his years with the Lions, he drew the analogy of Lindbergh's flight to Paris, and credited its success to his flying alone, saddled with no board of directors, "who knew nothing about flying, telling him what to do." Reaction around the league to the firing came quickly. George Marshall, owner of the Washington Redskins, growled, "What's the matter with the ownership? They didn't lose money last year — can't they stand prosperity?"

McMillin left behind an improved ball club with championship prospects. The 1950 season's six wins and six losses were a bigger mark of progress than the breakeven figures indicated. The crucial quarterback problem of recent seasons was solved with Layne, and the team showed new balance in both offensive and defensive capabilities. Only a few close games had kept the season from being outstanding. The Lions were now truly a McMillin team, for only one man remained from the 1947 low point. All the remainder of the 1950 Lions were his personal picks. Succeeding seasons proved the overwhelming success of his rebuilding work. He had created the nucleus of a championship team in Layne, Bingaman, Creekmur, Hart, Hoernschemeyer, McGraw, Prchlik, and Walker, one that drove to within one game of the title in '51, was World Champion in '52, '53 and Western Division winner in '54. McMillin's legacy was later readily admitted by the man who fired him, Anderson, and the player who opposed him, Layne. For so competitive a person, being fired was difficult enough, but to have it come when three years of work were about to be capped with success made a regretful situation an agonizing one. But he worked through it with the poise and fortitude he had always demonstrated.

When a defeated Bo McMillin had walked off the gridiron of Harvard Stadium in 1920, he sought another game with the Crimson to prove himself and his team. So now he left Detroit determined to find another football field on which to turn defeat into victory.

CHAPTER TEN

The Final Contest

(1950-1952)

To Bo, every undertaking had to be a challenge. Everything he achieved came the hard way, the way he seemed to want it.... As a coach, he never once enjoyed the luxury of being an assistant; he was always, from the start of his coaching career, the head man, the one who had to make the decisions and then stand on their merits.

Indiana Alumni Magazine

Bo McMillin's abrupt firing by the Lions left many of his friends and former associates convinced that his high moral standards were more responsible than his won-lost record. Stories began to circulate that he was too straitlaced for some of the directors, whose conduct on road trips he had criticized. Especially in Bloomington it became "gospel" that the Hoosier hero had been sacrificed for reasons unrelated to his coaching and recruiting ability.

After meeting a previously agreed to coaching commitment at the Senior Bowl in Mobile, he came home to find heartening coaching offers from the University of Detroit, Kansas State, and the Philadelphia Eagles. While a return to the familiar world of collegiate athletics may have been appealing, undoubtedly the challenge of another chance to prove himself in the professional ranks weighed heavily in his decision to sign on with the Eagles. He seemed unwilling to surrender the NFL to the standards set by Bobby Layne.

On 8 February, the Philadelphia papers reported the firing of the Eagles' head coach, Earle (Greasy) Neale, who had served since 1941. Out of consideration for Neale's feelings, McMillin insisted that this public announcement precede word of his own appointment.

Then, to make it official, at a luncheon in the Ritz-Carlton Hotel, he was formally introduced as the new Eagle head coach. Recollections of the difficult times of World War II intruded on his remarks as he expressed his misgivings: "It's hard to predict what's going to happen in these troubled days, but I hope I can get the best out of the material at hand." The worried reference to the dismal war news from Korea was understandable, but the absence of his usual enthusiasm and optimism less so. In retrospect it seems possible that persistent health problems were already taking a toll on his normally effusive attitude. Some close to him came to support this view, certain that even in Bo's last year with the Lions a lot of the warmth of character was gone, that he was probably a sick man at the time.

Although he had signed with the Eagles for three years at $15,000 per year, he would continue to collect his $30,000 per year from the Lions contract and unquestionably be the highest paid coach in pro ball. Newspaper articles carried pictures of the signing, hauntingly similar to the happy ones with the Lions exactly three years before. McMillin's sense of the unfinished surfaced as he told observers, "This gives me an opportunity to do something I didn't get a chance to do in Detroit." His old boss, Edwin Anderson, welcomed his return to the league, saying, "He's a top personality and a credit to football." In addition to the joy of remaining in football, Bo looked forward to reunion with his favorite player of the memorable Indiana days, big Pete Pihos, who was returning for his fifth season with the Eagles.

Along with McMillin's appointment, Vince McNally was named Eagle General Manager. And in a move to remove some of the fog that had led to so many misinterpretations of Bo's assignment in Detroit, the Eagles' president, James P. Clark, made it very plain that McNally would "have complete charge of player personnel. Vince and Bo will consult on player matters, but it will be Vince's responsibility to sign the players and Bo's to coach them." McMillin probably welcomed the change, for, as his friend Elden Auker observed, it was just too much, fighting salary problems, recruiting and buying players, and coaching the team as he had done with the Lions.

The retiring Philly coach, Greasy Neale, and McMillin had exactly the same 1950 record, 6-6. But while Bo's win-loss figure heralded a team on the way up, Neale's represented a collapse from the 11-1 record of the previous year, one serious enough to force the change.

Since the early forties the Eagles had been a tough team to play, and, for fans, an exciting one to watch. Now some critics clamored that the 1950 slump proved that they had grown old and tired. In other years they had been great, winning the 1947 Eastern Division title, and in 1948 and 1949 the NFC Championship. But these honors were memories; this was 1951 and McMillin would need all his skills of leadership and motivation to turn this sagging team around. The problem of a team in decline, however, mattered little to him; he was back, wooing his first love, football.

But a small cloud began to appear in Bo's sky. On a visit to Fort Worth in June, he addressed a group on the treatment of football injuries and some of those present noted that he appeared to be in less than robust health. The difference probably would not have been noticed but for his reputation for clean living and fine physical condition. Nevertheless, if he suffered, there is no record of his complaining to anyone about it. This was his way; he carried his own load.

By July, McMillin was getting letters from Eagle veterans telling him they were getting in shape "in parks, on golf courses, and back yards," that they planned to come in ready to play. The letters were written, perhaps, less from a revived enthusiasm for physical fitness than from their new coach's reputation as a taskmaster.

On Monday, 30 July, the squad left for its Hershey, Pennsylvania training site with fifty-three players signed, twenty-six of whom were newcomers. And in the manner of all incoming coaches, McMillin made it clear that all positions were open and had to be won. Characteristically, he began with an innovation, ordering the training of all players in both offense and defense. Disregarding some grumbling, he wanted a squad that could go both ways if necessary.

Early in the training camp, the *Inquirer* "Sportscope" made much of Bo's reputation among NFL players for being "a martinet and a slave driver." The article pointed to the reputed Lion player "revolt" as evidence and indicated that this image of the coach had preceded him. Nevertheless, the writer admitted that the reaction of the Eagles to his methods had been different. As one veteran expressed it, "McMillin has already won over even the 'hard heads'." He also expressed some amazement, saying, "Bo is a workhorse as a coach. Before the start of training, he spent hundreds of hours watching films of last year's games. He gave every player a rating for blocking, ball-carrying or pass catching. Thus he didn't come into training camp cold." The speaker would have been less surprised had he been familiar with Bo's total commitment to the principle of preparation.

During training camp some amusing evidences of Bo's frugality surfaced. Ed Hogan, the Eagles' publicity man, recalls once when the check came for a dinner McMillin had with some of his staff, Bo began meticulously dividing the bill among them. "Here was a guy wealthy enough to have bought the Eagles on his own, sweating over the dinner bill. Someone else grabbed and paid it." Another time, one of his staff recalled Bo carefully dividing twenty-five cent tolls and parking charges with his riders, explaining that he was "taking care of the gas and oil." The effects of the lean years of his boyhood never wore off.

In mid-August, the first exhibition game caused a flurry of renewed interest. In what was described as "a spectacular pass and run game," the Eagles showed new fight in rallying to beat the Pittsburgh Steelers, 24-9, after spotting them a 9-0 lead in the first quarter. Appreciative reviews of the game were upbeat and optimistic, calling the team the "New Philadelphia Eagles."

Then late in August on a steamy, hot and humid night at Shreveport, Louisiana, playing what most observers called a grudge match between Buddy Parker and McMillin, the Eagles battled the Detroit Lions to a 17-17 deadlock. Three times Philadelphia came from behind to finally get the tie. The feat loomed larger in light of the vastly improved Lions' recent victory over the 1950 World Champion Cleveland Browns. Emotions ran high as Buddy Parker displayed a bit of pre-game prima donna temperament, insisting unnecessarily on a change of dressing rooms and benches. The heat did little to cool tempers both on and off the field, and whatever this battle between McMillin and Parker was supposed to prove was lost in the disappointment of a sweaty tie.

Early September saw the Eagles beat the Packers 14-10 at the Mid-West Shrine game in Milwaukee. Frank O'Gara, the *Inquirer* sports writer assigned to the team, in recognition of the progress McMillin was making opined, "This is a team of championship caliber." Even if unduly enthusiastic, it was nice to read.

In the City of Philadelphia, no football game gets quite the media exposure as that given the *Inquirer's* Annual Charity Classic. To the

Philadelphia Inquirer this athletic event is topped only by the World Series, a subordination grudgingly admitted. This fourteenth year of the traditional event would pit the lean and mean Chicago Bears against the Eagles at the Municipal Stadium on 15 September, at 8 p.m. Part of the attendant hoopla was a Junior Chamber of Commerce football kickoff luncheon at the Bellevue Stratford Hotel, where McMillin told the faithful that every effort had been made to produce another title team. Again the zip was missing in his words, and again there were fears that something might be wrong.

The *Inquirer's* all-out publicity and McMillin's intensive team preparations for the Bears battle gave it local importance far beyond its status as an exhibition game. Traditionally, Philadelphia fans regarded the Bears as anathema, so the imperative for a win in this game had civic dimensions. McMillin, in his best country vernacular,told his team that they had to be "as high as Georgia pines" for the game, that the Bears would be their toughest opponent all year. For their part, the *Inquirer's* sportswriters dutifully whipped up local passions by describing the Eagles as "a fast-moving, explosive, pulse-racing team...[which] merits wholesale support," adding, "There is no doubt the veteran mentor [McMillin] is on the road to success in rebuilding the team." Evidence abounded that the silver-haired coach was capturing the imagination of Philadelphians.

To everyone's chagrin, and McMillin's embarrassment, the big event turned into a rout as the Bears "romped over the Eagles, 31-6." Forgetting the other successful pre-season games, one dour newspaper article headlined the disappointment, "Dismal debut for Bo." Then, like something better forgotten, the game quickly disappeared from the sports pages as fans went back to the World Series. Almost unnoticed, the Eagles went on to their last warm-up game with the New York Giants at Hershey Stadium where a small crowd saw them lose, 21-6. The exhibition season had started on a high note but finished disastrously. A worried coach had to get things turned around.

The Eagles opened their season with a 17-14 win over the St. Louis Cardinals. However, while the team seemed up and stronger, Bo seemed less than fit. Not arriving until half-time, he blamed food poisoning from his seafood dinner the night before for his tardiness. Obviously not well, without real protest, he allowed the team physician to banish him to the press-box. Permitting himself to be removed from the action was an awesome sign and testified to the severity of his problem. Unsuspecting writers, with some amusement, reported how he "hopped around the press box," frustrated and impatient with his isolation. At the second game in Shibe Park, he was back on the sidelines with his hat-twisting, nerve-wracking intensity as the Eagles whipped the San Francisco 49ers, 21-14. But now the strain was clearly too much for him. McMillin finally had to admit that he was very ill. The following Monday he was in the hospital to find out what was wrong.

The answer came quickly. On Friday the newspapers headlined "Operation today for Eagle pilot," an "intestinal disorder" the reputed cause. In recognition of the seriousness of his condition, he said his goodbyes to the team, for it was patently clear that he would not be back soon. An exploratory operation confirmed what must have been a lingering worry in McMillin's mind; it was cancer of the stomach. The grim verdict carried a shattering corollary that was difficult to accept — the doctors ordered him out of football. He simply could not stand the intense strain he always underwent on the sidelines. In a personal tragedy like this a man's inner thoughts seldom find their way into print, but it is not difficult to guess his. Handed so poor a prognosis on the one hand, and denied the joy of his beloved football on the other, McMillin's world had collapsed.

The suddenness of the onset of the disease shocked everyone, but some of those close to the coach began to recall that there had been signs. During the previous fall, Edwin Anderson had noticed a change in Bo. He felt something of his natural warmth toward his players was missing. An especially fine play by "his boys" brought none of his usual praise or comment. When asked about it, he had replied, rather testily, that they were paid to perform. Some players, too, when they thought about it, also felt that there had been indications that their coach was a sick man in that last Lion season. They could point to nothing specific, but most agreed that he had not seemed well. Perhaps in retrospect, they were reading things that were not there, but so many noticed that it seems likely Bo's natural ebullience had been missing.

The Eagles at first refused to name a new head coach, simply installing Bo's assistant, Wayne Milner, veteran professional player and star from Notre Dame, to handle the team "till Bo was able to return." The gesture was well-intended, but when subsequent prognoses by the surgeons turned so pessimistic, Clark named Milner head coach for the remainder of the season, saying, "It is a keen disappointment that we will lose Bo's services this season, but if it will contribute to his return to good health, that alone is a real consolation." His return to health, however, would take more than words and rest; it would take a miracle. McMillin was backed up on his own goal line and it was fourth down.

Not that he resigned himself to defeat by his illness; he could not. All his life he had battled the odds and, more often than not, won. Spirit and desire, he firmly believed, were the essentials of victory. But this time he fought an implacable enemy which knew no retreat. When, in late winter, McMillin visited the Eagles' office, he was a shadow. Those who saw him were pained to realize that it was the same man who "had his share of vanity, maybe sometimes more than his share," who had always been proud of his physical condition, of his "hard, flat stomach" and "legs that bulged and rippled like a ballet dancer even when he was 57." He had wasted away; he was down to 110 pounds. Only indomitable courage and an abiding religious faith kept this shell battling.

"Look at my legs," he hoarsely whispered, "They have shrunk away to nothing. All I can do is to keep on praying and praying that I will recover my health and strength."

When he was strong enough, he made the trip to Detroit's Henry Ford Hospital for further treatment and perhaps surcease from the constant pain that wracked him. He had reached the stage in the disease when pain made him willing to try anything to find relief. He was attracted to a clinic in Windsor, Canada where a doctor enjoyed some success in relieving cancer patients in severe pain, and went there for three weeks or so for treatment. His old player and friend over the years, Elden Auker, visited him daily while there and tells a story that beautifully illustrates the monumental faith and spirit that filled McMillin.

Each day Auker met Bo's priest at his church for the trip to the clinic, pre-warned that there could be no conversation until after he had given the daily communion to their sick friend. Auker would wait outside the room as the priest gave the ritual bread, wine, and expiation to him. On one occasion, coming from the sick room, the priest mused that although religion was his "business," Bo made him feel like "an amateur," so great was his belief and faith. The priest averred that if anyone could survive cancer, he was convinced that Bo could. Once when Auker went into the room after the priest had just left, McMillin brightened and confided that each time he had taken communion he would have absolutely no pain for two hours afterwards. Then it would come surging back and he could hardly stand it. But the brief respite stood as testimony to the strength of a life-long faith he had lived and practiced. And, like the fighter he was, he grimly promised, "Cancer will never kill me!"

After the Windsor Clinic interlude, McMillin returned to Ford Hospital for another six weeks, but time was running out; he was deteriorating badly. As his disease advanced, the family agreed with his desire to return to Indiana. When Auker carried him to the plane that General Motors Corporation provided for the trip back to Bloomington, he sadly noted that McMillin had wasted away to sixty pounds; he was a wraith.

He had left Indiana for Detroit's big money, but his illness reminded him that his heart was still in Bloomington. There were the close friends of years, there the aura of the glory days at Indiana University, there the memories of the hundreds of "boys" who had felt his magic, there the honored place he had won in the hearts of so many, and there, even more than Texas, was "home." In November the McMillins moved back to an apartment in Bloomington and, in early January, established permanent residence as they bought a new home there.

Here, surrounded by the familiar past, things seemed as they had been — the warmth, the caring, the constant visits of old friends. Bo was still hero, still the "Coach," still the only man to bring an undefeated season and a Big Ten Football championship to Indiana. Just a month before he died, he wrote his old friend Chief Myers the words characterizing his life-long habit of fighting the odds: "They tell me that my condition is desperate. I can still remember from boyhood your instructions were to fight until the last whistle blew. Rugged as it is, I plan to do just that."

One honor that final winter cheered him. The American Football Coaches Association awarded him the prestigious Amos Alonzo Stagg Trophy for his contributions to the game. The presentation properly acknowledged a lifetime playing and coaching career made noteworthy by his dedication to the promotion of collegiate sport. He had every reason to be proud of this recognition from his peers; the tough little kid from Prairie Hill, Texas, had come a long way. Another gift pleased the desperately ill Bo when the Detroit Lions presented him with the game ball from their winning division championship game, a thoughtful acknowledgement that his rebuilding efforts had put them there.

In February, he entered the Bloomington Hospital not for cure, but in hope of respite. The will was still vital and strong, but the flesh was mortal. A welcomed visitor at Bo's bedside was his friend of so many years, "Happy" Chandler. During their long and warm conversation, the pain and loneliness of Bo's condition became acutely apparent. He told Happy, "We've had a good life, had lots of fun, but I'm a goner. These doctors are great, but they can't do anything for me. I don't mind, except that the nights are so long." These poignant words inscribed themselves so indelibly in Chandler's memory that he had no trouble repeating them more than thirty years later. Others came, more to say goodbye than in hope of cheering. Old time friends like Matty Bell, Lou Little, Ed Diddle, "Tuss" McLaughery, and Jim Trimble visited. Many unable to drop by sent their best wishes: Harry Stuhldreher, Fritz Crisler, Wallace Wade, Amos Alonzo Stagg, Carl Snavely, Bob Neyland and so many more. Ten former rival collegiate coaches, while attending the NCAA meeting in Cincinnati, phoned him words of encouragement. The Football Rules Committee sent him a treasured memento, a football autographed by most of the famous names in the sport. The outpouring of affection and concern must have cheered him. His boyhood chum, "Cow" Minton, made the journey to Bloomington and left visibly shaken after seeing McMillin's condition and the unrelenting pain his close friend suffered.

On 21 March they sent him home, for McMillin seemed to have rallied a bit and those around him were encouraged. The following Tuesday, another friend from the past came to see Bo and relive old times. Norris Armstrong, captain of the famed 1921 Centre College team that beat Harvard, brought with him shining memories of those golden days. On his last Sunday evening Bo enjoyed a long talk with Howard Brown, his rugged lineman of the great Indiana team, as they refought the happy battles of years ago. A few hours after Brown left, in the sleepless, restless early morning of 31 March 1952, at 2:30 a.m., Bo began to weaken, and the courageous heart that had fought so long and so hard against a savaging disease finally gave out. With his loved ones gathered round him, Alvin Nugent McMillin lay dead of a heart attack at fifty-seven. True to his prediction dreaded cancer had not killed him. His family had lost a devoted father and husband, and football, a legend and champion.

The tributes began pouring into Bloomington as the great names of football began to gather. Indiana University's president and long time friend of McMillin, Herman Wells, said, "All who knew Bo loved him. The warmth of his personality was irresistible. He possessed rare qualities of wit, loyalty and courage in abundance. As a leader of young men he was unexcelled. The University community is deeply saddened by his untimely passing." The evening before the funeral, a rosary was recited at the Allen Funeral Home, where the body was lying in state. McMillin would have liked that, for his devout Catholic faith had been his daily rule and guide, as well as a staunch ally throughout his wasting illness.

Thursday, 3 April at 10 a.m., at a requiem mass in the crowded sanctuary of St. Charles Catholic Church, old friends and long time associates gathered in sad farewell. There were more floral pieces than anyone could ever recall. One account mentioned that four trucks were needed to carry flowers to the gravesite. One floral piece in particular that struck deep chords of memory had come from the Harvard Athletic Association. The flower-filled altar testified to a lifetime of service and the bonds of many friendships. The list of honorary pallbearers included distinguished names that covered the length of Bo's long and colorful career. A group of selected voices from Schola Cantorum of S.S. Peter and Paul Cathedral of Indianapolis sang responses to Father English. There was no eulogy, but Msgr. Thomas J. Kilfoil closed the service, saying, "We may learn a lot about God through the death of Mr. McMillin. He lived in simple faith. He obeyed the laws of God, because he loved God and therefore he served God. It may be said of him: 'I have run the race; I have fought the fight; I have kept the faith.' "

His old football players of the glory years, Howard Brown, Pete Pihos, Vernon Huffman, Robert Ravensburg, Russell Deal, and Elden Auker carried Bo's massive cherry casket to a "gently sloping hillside" in the Rose Hill Cemetery "near a spreading tree under bright spring skies." And there, in simple dignity, he was laid to rest. In final tribute, across the grave lay a blanket of 1500 carnations in Indiana's colors, cream and crimson, a remembrance from the Indiana Varsity Lettermen's Club, and appropriately, one of Bo's old linemen, florist John Olmstead, had designed it.

The funeral was an emotional reunion for his former players. As happens at such times, conversations drifted into heart-tugging reminiscences, such as Jim Trimble's with Bo's old center, "Red" Roberts. Roberts told of having a twisted and broken little finger on his right hand which Bo claimed affected his centering the ball. In all seriousness, Bo had recommended that he have it cut off to improve his ball control. Together they chuckled at the familiar intensity of Bo, but in parting, Trimble's surprise must have been obvious as he felt Roberts' three-fingered handshake.

In recognition that football had lost one of its greats, newspapers around the nation printed column after column of obituary, recollections, and tributes. In most, the Harvard-Centre game of 1921 was relived for a new generation. But of all the words written on the death of Bo McMillin, he might have been best satisfied with a simple line from the *New York Times* obituary, describing him as "one of football's immortals and a man who loved the game and the boys who play it."

The Measure Of The Man

Bo McMillin had lived for football since that day in 1912 when he had put on his first uniform for North Side High School. Only his family had held an equal place in his life. On his deathbed, he spent long, pain-filled hours reflecting on his forty years as a player and coach. To Matty Bell, Norris Armstrong, Rosco Minton, and other former teammates and friends, he expressed his fears of a rapidly growing professionalism threatening to ruin the game to which he had given his life.

His love of football, he believed, had retrieved him from a life headed nowhere and given it purpose, or as he liked to say, had kept him "from becoming a tramp." He worried now as he saw the sport entering a new era in which more and more boys played for financial rewards — either a scholarship or outright pay — and the chance of becoming a professional after college, rather than for the pure love of the game that had motivated his teammates at North Side High School and Centre College. Poignant memories of those days when they had turned the vision of Chief Myers into reality brought brief respites from pain and moments of fleeting hope that God would spare his life so he might launch a crusade to save college football by restoring its pristine spirit and values.

He found in his own memories reason to be concerned about the game. His playing days and first coaching years had not been free from the evils of the sport, so widely denounced by its critics. After five years on high school gridirons, he had gone to college to play foot-ball, not to study, as his grades and failure to graduate make evident. Centre surely stretched the still nebulous eligibility regulations to keep its greatest player on the field. It is difficult to accept fully this proud little college's protestations that academic pursuits were not secondary during the glory years of 1917 to 1921. Perhaps no college's future ever hung more precariously on the success of its football team than did Centenary's during McMillin's stay there. And he could not deny that he had left college to take the best offer he received. But the wiser, mature Bo wanted better for his "pore lil' boys." He set an example by going back to school to earn his degree, and he never ceased to preach that others must profit from his experience. Now in his final days he was tormented with thoughts of carousing Bobby Layne setting standards of conduct for both professional and college players, of universities becoming farm teams of the NFL, and of more and more boys putting on the pads for pay from alumni who demanded a winner.

Sport for this Texas lad had been a spiritual experience. Although remaining a lifelong, devout Catholic, he was perfectly at home in Protestant Middle America, and he sincerely believed that football inculcated the values of this society as did no other influence outside the churches. The game became for him a quasi religion of which he was an evangelist. He preached this faith not only to his players but in hundreds of "pulpits" provided by invitations for the "Praying Colonel" to speak. His message never varied: through clean living, self-discipline, hard work, courage, sportsmanship, and loyalty to teammates, boys of even mediocre athletic ability could succeed in both athletics and life. As a legendary example of the redeeming power of the sport, he could preach with conviction that football could do for others what it had done for him. Like many converts to a new faith, his zeal may have led him to exaggerate somewhat the "sinfulness" of the life from which he had been saved. But such overcoloring of his early years served his purpose well and enhanced his legend.

Legends often fade with the passage of time. The year after his death Centre College dedicated with great fanfare the "McMillin Memorial Room," a chamber dominated by a nearly life sized portrait of Bo in his college uniform. Yet when Centre erected a new athletic building a generation later, the McMillin Room disappeared. He is better remembered at Indiana University, where a plaque in the center of the school's Hall of Fame commemorates his Big Ten championship. His most lasting monument, however, has remained in the hearts and minds of those who knew him, as their enthusiastic contributions to this biography attest.

McMillin came to fame as a player at the opening of the 1920s, a decade that produced successive waves of heroes in sport and other fields. His two climactic performances in Harvard Stadium could only temporarily hold the attention of a society that sought a constant supply of new heroes. By spending his first six years as a coach in small colleges he preserved his self-image but narrowed the circle of his influence. Then during the lean seasons at Kansas State and Indiana he provided an admirable example of how a coach can balance the conflicting pressures to win and also be an educator, primarily concerned with the self-development of those students under his direction. However he ranks in the list of all-time gridiron greats, he had few equals as both an advocate and practitioner of those values that for more than a century Americans have seen in their unique game of football.

New York Times columnist Arthur Daly eulogized McMillin the coach as "a true builder of character," but added, "the best job he did in that respect was in building his own." As Chief Myers, one of the honorary pallbearers, followed Bo's casket out of St. Charles Church, he understood better than anyone else the meaning of such a tribute. Myers's grief was surely eased by pride in having introduced football to North Side High School forty years before.

Index